THE ART OF
GARDENING WITH ROSES

THE ART OF GARDENING WITH ROSES

Graham Stuart Thomas

With Photographs by Bob Gibbons

A John Macrae Book
Henry Holt and Company
New York

Published in the United States by
Henry Holt and Company, Inc., 115 West 18th Street,
New York, New York 10011

Library of Congress Catalog Card Number: 90-5377

ISBN 0-8050-1533-7

Henry Holt books are available at special discounts
for bulk purchases for sales promotions, premiums,
fund-raising, or educational use. Special editions
or book excerpts can also be created to specification.

For details contact:
Special Sales Director
Henry Holt and Company, Inc.
115 West 18th Street
New York, New York 10011

First American Edition

Printed and bound in Hong Kong

Recognizing the importance of preserving
the written word, Henry Holt and Company, Inc.,
by policy, prints all of its first editions
on acid-free paper. ∞

3   5   7   9   10   8   6   4   2

Frontispiece

'JEAN BODIN'

The Moss rose 'Jean Bodin' was raised in France and named in 1843. It has brownish young leaves turning later to deep leaden green, on an upright, self-reliant bush, which will probably reach to about 4 ft (1.2m). Few roses present their blooms better; they are arranged all over the bushes, almost from the ground upwards and they are interspersed with clusters of buds covered with brownish moss. The moss is of the rather stiff, prickly kind inherited from the Perpetual White Damask Moss. Like almost all Moss roses this has a delicious scent. This plant, being backed by a cool shady wall, is underplanted with *Viola cornuta alba*, a true perennial, hardy, wild *Viola* which is available in soft purple, light lilac and pure white. They can easily be increased by division in spring but also usually breed true from seeds. They should be planted on the shady side of bushes, where they will be more healthy and flower longest; in moist seasons from June until autumn. Here they have scrambled up through 'Jean Bodin's' branches.

To his many associates and friends
who have helped to realize this project and especially to
David G. Stone and his colleagues
who have created order out of chaos
by their interest and industry
this book is dedicated by
the author.

'ANEMONE' (*overleaf, page 8*)

One of the earliest roses to flower every year is the Anemone rose. Because it is slightly tender it is grown on a warm sunny wall where its blooms are hastened, heralding the rose season. It is a sparse grower and needs little pruning, just a thinning of old wood after flowering and subsequent tying-in of new shoots. A full- grown plant should reach 15 ft (4.5m) high and wide. But be chary about doing too much pruning; it is a rose all on its own, and frequently produces odd later blooms after the late spring flush. This is because one of its parents is thought to be a Tea rose; it owes its lovely glossy leaves to *R. laevigata*, the Cherokee Rose, so called because, though a native of China, it has colonized areas of Georgia, U.S.A., and is there adopted as the State's own flower. As to the Tea rose parent, this will obviously have been one of the Tea hybrids of early days with some of the China rose in its blood; this is because of its pink colouring (the Wild Tea rose, *Rosa gigantea*, is palest yellow) and the darker, true crimson staining at the edge of some of the petals. After all these details of culture and parentage it must be given its rightful name of *R.* 'Anemone' (synonym *R. anemonoides*), the Anemone Rose, raised at Erfurt in 1895. And for those who like stronger colours there is its ''sport'' in cerise crimson, 'Ramona', contrasted by the backs of the petals in grey-white. It occurred in California in 1913.

Contents

Foreword

MORE THAN ANYBODY else, Graham Stuart Thomas launched the revival of interest in roses long out of favor or commerce.

Many of the most valued and largely unheard of roses of the nineteenth century he acquired from America and France. He found many at the old Bobbink and Atkins Nursery in New Jersey and the old Lester and Tillotson rose nursery in California.

Interest in the old-fashioned kinds of roses — the albas, damasks, centifolias and gallicas — had never fully died out since those varieties were popular in the past century (most of them were Victorian, rather than ancient) and even as the flood of new roses with Chinese blood swept across the gardening world, especially after 1850, there were occasional pleas not to forget the older varieties.

But gardeners then as now were enchanted with roses that bloomed from May till November, and when these began to appear, thanks to Chinese genes for repeat-flowering roses, few gardeners continued to make room for the oldsters that bloomed only in spring.

In the American South, and along the Mediterranean shores, the old Noisettes and Teas, that bloomed steadily through the growing season until quite hard freezes temporarily stopped them, remained not only popular but veritable mainstays of the garden, especially in country gardens and among the poor who had little access to the newer kinds from Europe.

But the Noisettes and Teas were of no comfort in the chillier temperate regions, as they were severely injured not only by temperatures of fifteen degrees or below, but also by prolonged cold spells at higher temperatures

A number of writers and growers called for a revival of interest in old roses before Graham Stuart Thomas, and he freely built on their labors and on the interest they had aroused. All the same, it was not until Mr. Thomas began to collect these antiques passionately at his Sunningdale Nurseries, and began to write about them in the journals of the Royal Horticultural Society and in his books, that the gardening world at large sat up and took notice.

At the time the oldest garden roses were popular, before the reign of Victoria, a gardener had far fewer ornamental plants available to him than he had later in the century, as witnessed by Thomas's Mottisfont garden described and illustrated in this valuable book. The rise of garden magazines, the sudden abundance of nurseries that catered to the middle classes, the continuing abundance of new plants arriving from all over the world, the relative cheapness of glass houses and labor, all served to excite gardeners who were now aware of new wonders to acquire and grow.

Roses had greater competition, in other words, for space; and when varieties appeared that bloomed over a period of five months instead of two or three weeks, they were given the space once devoted only to the spring-blooming sorts.

But he who feasts every day feasts no day, as the old adage goes. If the old roses had been just like the new kinds except for a briefer flowering season, they never would have been revived and glorified, as they are today. But they were quite different in shape, color and (in many cases) perfume.

Besides, some of the old kinds such as the Albas, excelled not only in scent but in toughness. No winter kills them to the ground. No miserable weather in spring causes them to ball or mildew. In hot steamy summers they are not defoliated by black spot. And in all springs they bear their blue-grey-green leaves distinctively, and their neat salver flowers with the petals swirling as if in a whirlpool were easily distinguished from the newer roses. They did not have every charm or every merit, but what they had was distinctly different.

Mr. Thomas's contributions to the revival of interest in all classes of old roses rest not only on his commercial efforts to raise and sell them, in the years he was in the nursery business, but even more importantly on three books, *The Old Shrub Roses*, *Shrub Roses of Today*, and *Climbing Roses Old and New*. As gardeners soon discovered, it was necessary to have all three volumes, as gaps in one volume were tended to in another, and never mind the individual title.

Especially valuable, I thought, was *Climbing Roses Old and New*, as the old climbers were even more neglected than the old bush roses. To give an example, the Noisette climber, 'Jaune Desprez' of 1831, was once one of the most prized roses in America, France and England. It was a favorite rose of Robert Buist, who sold it at his famous old nursery in Philadelphia. But it was not to be found in rose nurseries of America (or elsewhere) for many years until Mr. Thomas once again called attention to its superlative merits in gardens of moderate climates.

The authority of Graham Stuart Thomas is by no means limited to roses. He has written authoritatively on perennials, garden design, the grouping of plants, on groundcovers and much else, as the reader of this delightful book will discover. Indeed, sometimes he has resented the notion, popular among rose fanatics, that since he is the czar of old roses, he must grow nothing else. On the contrary, few gardeners are so catholic or such plant connoisseurs.

Many gardeners simply focus on roses and ignore everything else. Surely they can be forgiven for their lack of balance as they have been tempted beyond mere mortal endurance by Mr. Thomas's three rose books. And now, with this further volume on the great rose collection of Mottisfont Abbey (of which Mr. Thomas is of course the father) with his further discussion of particular varieties, and superb colour pictures of them those gardeners who had devoted only four-fifths of their space to roses will probably now intrude further on their viburnums and lilacs (already in precarious security as the tide of old roses has swept over them) to make room for more.

In time, the fanatics for old roses will strike a balance. There is no revolution in which blood is not shed. If Mr. Thomas more or less single-handedly has caused old roses to become an obsession with many gardeners, at least there are few plants so deserving of reckless admiration. His championing of the Portland roses alone — and this is only one group he has brought to the consciousness of all gardeners — justifies the regard in which rose enthusiasts hold him. One eagerly awaits yet another volume.

Henry Mitchell
Washington, D.C.
May, 1990

The Art of Designing a Rose Garden

You violets that first appeare,
By your pure purple mantles known,
Like the proud virgins of the yeare,
As if the spring were all your owne,
What are you when the Rose is blown?

Sir Henry Wotton, 1568–1639

P EOPLE INSTINCTIVELY LOVE gardens designed for roses — our favourite
hardy flower. It is a tradition to have a pattern of beds in lawn or
paving; this tradition has arisen from the fact that modern roses
provide low colour over many weeks, thus being favourites for filling the
beds which had their origin in the parterres of the seventeenth century.
But few plants are further removed from their wild originals than our
modern roses.

A botanist would tell you that there are some 150 species wild in the
Northern Hemisphere; some as low as 1ft (30cm), others ascending to 60ft
(18m). Of these the vast majority are of pink or mauve with a few white;
yet a few more are of pale yellow, from Asia. Any tint of red is confined
to one Chinese species and to abnormal "sports" of two species that are
normally pink or brilliant yellow.

Very few of these species from the wild have given rise to our modern
garden roses. In fact gardens in Europe before 1800 were almost entirely
peopled with ancient hybrids of a mere four species, all natives of southern
Europe and the Near East, together with Sweet Brier and the Scotch Rose
and a few more. These were all in tones of pink. In China only two species,
a red and a pale yellow, became hybridized likewise in antiquity, four of
the hybrids having reached Europe between 1792 and 1824, comprising
two pink, one pale yellow and one crimson. These became hybridized with
the Europeans during the nineteenth century with the result that garden
roses by 1900 embraced crimson, purple, lilac, pink, white and pale yellow,
with a few of apricot or peach tint — the mixing of the pale yellow with
the pinks. Just prior to 1900 a hybrid was raised in France combining the
brilliant sulphur-yellow of the Persian Yellow rose with the soft mauve-
crimson of the old European garden roses. Soon the Persian Yellow's sport,
the so-called Austrian Copper, of a bright tomato-red, was brought into
bearing and colours became much more vivid, enhanced by a curious
happening: in 1929 a new colour occurred as a sport (pelargonidin — a

'GOLDFINCH'

Our mixed borders at Mottisfont are mostly peopled with short growing plants to enable the visitor to see across them to the small lawns surrounded with roses. To give height at regular intervals are Rambler roses supported by panels of woodwork. They are composed of riven timber which lasts longer than when sawn. Two uprights and some crossbars support the creamy yellow 'Goldfinch', an almost thornless rose of *R. multiflora* derivation, named in 1907 when raised by George Paul of Cheshunt, England, who was famous for several good roses, such as his 'Paul's Lemon Pillar', 'Tea Rambler' and 'Una'. As companions in the picture there are pale pink pyrethrums (*Tanacetum coccineum* 'Eileen May Robinson') and the glorious blue of *Veronica austriaca* (*V. teucrium*) 'Royal Blue', while to bring in firmness of outline and solidity there is the tall *Iris* 'Ochraurea' and the leaves of *Bergenia cordifolia* 'Purpurea'. The iris is one of the best and most imposing of the Spuria group which flower after the usual Bearded or German irises, and have dramatically shaped, long-lasting flowers coupled with superior, tall foliage.

---

very vivid orange-red). With this addition modern roses have assumed ever brighter colours.

The trend of fashion, fostered by rosarians and rose-breeders alike, through the last 200 years or so, has been towards plants which will give bright colours over a long period. It is a strange fact that these have been bred from such a tiny handful of species, leaving so many species untapped.

It is mainly among what we may call the European ancestral hybrids and their derivatives that I have devoted much time since before the Second World War, trying to recapture the appearance of a collection of roses of the late nineteenth century. They were of white, mauve-pink and purplish crimson tints and were stalwart hardy bushes, mostly very fragrant. From China the pale yellow, rather tender climber gave rise to the early yellowish climbing Noisette and other roses; the dark crimson was a weakling and only slowly deepened the colours. Therefore in re-creating a garden composed of these old roses there are three important factors to be taken to heart. There are the colours of the flowers borne mostly on big vigorous shrubs often over 4ft (1.2m) in height and width; the flowering season which is limited to three or four weeks at midsummer except with a few varieties; there were also a few graceful ramblers but these were of pale colouring.

12

'HARISON'S YELLOW'

Vivid colouring at the beginning of the long mixed borders which extend from the entrance right through the centre of the rose garden. In the picture is the brilliant sulphur-yellow of *Rosa x harisonii* or 'Harison's Yellow', raised in New York in 1830. This is a hybrid of the Scots Brier with *Rosa foetida*, the so-called Austrian Brier. The supposition that the latter rose was in the parentage of Harison's rose is confirmed by its heavy smell, not the fresh fragrance of the Scots Brier. It is a thorny bush reaching to about 5ft (1.5m) and requires no pruning beyond the removal, immediately after flowering, of a few old, weak, twiggy shoots. It ushers in the rose season with verve and brilliance, here grouped with an early scarlet peony, *Paeonia peregrina* 'Fire King', the straw-pale yellow spires of *Sisyrinchium striatum* and the old Bearded Iris, 'Iris King', dating from 1907. The *Sisyrinchium* (see also page 47) seeds itself all over the place but has a long flowering period and its cool colour blends with anything, while its iris-like foliage (it is a close relative of the irises) is attractive for many weeks.

Given that colours other than green are dominant in most garden scheming, we have before us that fundamental division of hues so important in successful associations: while the old roses are almost all on the blue side, the moderns are on the yellow side of the reds and pinks in the spectrum. To those sensitive to colours the two simply do not blend. It is the same in the genus *Rhododendron* in which there are fiery reds, oranges and strong yellows that fight with the pinks and mauves and crimsons. Later in the season similar clashes of colour occur when seeking to combine hydrangeas, fuchsias and Japanese anemones with the many orange-yellow daisy flowers and montbretias.

Though the old roses tend to flower but once, the moderns may bloom from midsummer till autumn. But here comes another thought: would you rather have a small bush producing, say, up to 100 flowers over three or four months or a large shrub giving 200 or so blooms over three or four weeks? It has been said there are roses for all tastes. To demand of roses that they shall flower from summer until autumn has become second nature. Perhaps we have been spoiled. We do not expect this of our daffodils, irises, peonies and lilacs. Is there not sufficient variety for us to enjoy flowers in season, to be ready to welcome the next in the pageant of beauty through the summer?

When in full flower, a big wild rose — such as our native Dog Brier — and all the great shrub roses of the nineteenth century produce a somewhat spotty effect, the dotting of the flowers all over the shrub and the comparatively small divided foliage both contribute to this. These result in a frothy display which can only be taken in moderation. They need the steadying power of smooth lawns, paths and hedges and a sober underplanting. While it is my opinion that shrub roses are supremely beautiful and should dominate their places in the garden, they need a good blend of companion shapes and colours and should not be overdone.

With regard to ramblers and climbers, much enjoyment can be obtained from training them on walls, pillars and arches, but however much training and care may be given them, those of graceful growth do not reveal their greatest beauty and joy until one can contemplate the falling spray. Then and then only do these roses reveal their ultimate charm.

Into the art of arranging a rose garden must be brought the practicalities. Though the older shrub roses are remarkably thrifty and mostly long-lived, they root deeply and demand thorough and deep digging prior to planting. No rose will do well in an average hole dug in an old garden border. It is a known fact that no members of the Rose Family — roses, apples, plums, etc. — grow well in soil previously used by one of the genera; the soil should be replaced or sterilized. Gardeners wish that roses were not prickly; the prickles are produced for defence and also as a means in the wild of helping to hoist the branches into the sun, for they are all ardent sun lovers. The prickles prove that in the wild roses surmount other growths and thus prefer to grow where the soil is cool and sheltered from the sun. From this I deduce that they are not so dependent upon large doses of nitrogenous manures as they are on fertilizers containing plenty of phosphate and potash. Richly mulched with peat, leafmould, bark or garden compost and fed with a balanced fertilizer, the unsightly black spot and debilitating rust (prevalent in some seasons) will be less insidious. Mildew is more often caused by dry soil and damp air than by soil deficiencies.

The vast majority of roses are propagated by nurserymen 'budding' the leaf-eyes onto easily reproduced root-stocks. This is the best method to ensure a uniform crop. The union of scion and stock should be planted just below the level of the ground. If and when the rootstock produces a 'sucker' it is useless to cut it off: it will simply duplicate itself. It must be pulled off at the point of growth from the root; this entails uncovering the root and giving a pull with a gloved hand or a claw-headed hammer. Sometimes the presence of such suckers prompts the longing for roses on their own roots. Believe me, roses of the Gallica, Alba and Rugosa groups in particular are extremely prone to sending up their own suckers yards away from the plants, and can be a persistent nuisance.

14

The First Rose Garden

He who would have beautiful roses in his garden
must have beautiful roses in his heart.

Dean Hole, A *Book about Roses*, 1870

W E ARE NOW at the garden door. Few better sites could have been
found for a garden of old roses than this. It is roughly square
with cross-paths meeting at the central pool and fountain
guarded by eight Irish Yews. Following the line of the old soft-toned, red-
brick walls are gravel walks hedged with box. In the middle of each quarter
of the whole plot is a small rectangular lawn. There were several old apple
trees which make good hosts for climbers. The main path from the garden
door leads to an arch in the distant wall and the whole walk is given
almost entirely to four borders of hardy plants of soft colours. Only at the
very beginning of the borders are a few strong colours allowed to give point
to the general scheme. Tall plants are kept to the beginnings and ends and
around the junction at the pool where four Sweet Briers are planted in
order to stop the eye from taking in too great a length at once and also
to give warm fragrance from the foliage to those occupying the seats —
and, of course, the added bonus of the glittering scarlet heps in autumn.
The pool is decorated with one plant of a modern rose, 'Raubritter' in
clear pink; no other rose that I know would so exactly fulfil its purpose
— an off-centrepiece to the whole garden.

Originally there were several old clumps of peonies, bearded irises,
pyrethrums, erigerons and phloxes which were kept and incorporated in
the new planting plan. With some alpine phloxes, aubrietas, *Alyssum*
(*Aurinia*) *saxatile* 'Citrinum', bulbous irises and tulips the borders bring
some early colour to the garden echoed in the rose borders by more dwarf
early plants including *Saponaria ocymoides* and lots of seed-raised pinks in
white and tones of pink, often with maroon centres, together with the
lavender-blue and white of *Campanula carpatica*.

While the tradition of central borders of flowers has for long been the
decoration of a kitchen garden, I did not want it to assume too great an
importance in what was to be principally a garden of roses. The majority
of hardy plants were therefore chosen for their short height and long-
flowering habits, so that over them could be seen the small lawns
surrounded by roses. Height is given by some pillars of rambler roses placed
at regular intervals where the borders abut onto the lawns, with a firm
edging of bergenias and *Kniphofia caulescens*. Taller plants and some

15

Buddleja 'Lochinch' surround the bases of the pillars and, echoing their position in the borders, there are standard specimens of varieties of *Hibiscus syriacus* for late summer display. The whole of the main areas of the borders are filled with clumps of dense-growing hardy plants and a few dwarf shrubs to give a continuous display of low, soft colour which, at rose time, is mainly white, blue, lavender and pale yellow. Pinks and crimsons occur later. The fact that most of the plants are of short growth means economy in staking.

Among the shorter plants are *Centaurea hypoleuca* 'John Coutts' noted for its greyish leaves and long succession of pink "Sweet Sultan" flowers, crimson Clove Carnations, Catmint, the dark purple spikes of *Salvia nemorosa* 'East Friesland' and blue, pink and white Hyssop. The vertical line, though still short, is given by the straw-yellow *Sisyrinchium striatum* and silvery *Stachys byzantina (S. olympica)* or "Lambs Ears". For rather later and long-continuing display are the nemophila-blue *Geranium wallichianum* 'Buxton's Variety', the white "ever-lasting" flowers of *Anaphalis triplinervis* and lavender-blue daisies of *Aster thomsonii* 'Nanus'. Richer colour follows from the plum-crimson *Penstemon* 'Garnet' and *Fuchsia magellanica* 'Thompsonii', the daintiest of the shorter growing hardy fuchsias, in crimson with purple 'skirt'. Lighting all these plants in later summer is the pale yellow *Crocosmia* x *crocosmiiflora* which we all know, erroneously, as 'Citronella', and over a goodly clump of leaves are the stalwart erect stems of *Phlomis russeliana*, bearing whorls of soft butter-yellow hooded flowers. We hoped to grow both blue and white forms of *Scabiosa caucasica* but they have not been easy to establish. *Stokesia laevis* provides large blue flowers and the same colouring is forthcoming from *Eryngium* x *tripartitum*, very long-lasting and drought-resisting, and from *Agapanthus* Headbourne Hybrids. These are for late summer.

It will be appreciated that none of the above plants impedes the view over the wide borders to the little lawns. Rather taller plants at the ends of the borders are the cool yellow *Achillea* 'Flowers of Sulphur' which fades to a soft parchment tint, clouds of the common *Gypsophila paniculata*, the lavender-blue spikes and grey leaves of the best of all the Russian Sage hybrids, *Perovskia* 'Blue Spire', and the soft pink of the earliest flowering of the Japanese Anemones 'September Charm'. Sprawling on the ground is *Knautia macedonica* (*Scabiosa rumelica*), its rich crimson daisies vieing in beauty with the equally sprawling herbaceous *Clematis heracleifolia* 'Wyevale' in hyacinth-blue (the flowers are like those of hyacinths too), and palest yellow *Centaurea ruthenica*, a Knapweed of special elegance and beauty, stiffly upstanding.

I mentioned earlier that at the extreme ends of the borders really large plants are used: big banks of blue *Echinops ritro*, the early white clouds of the giant Seakale, *Crambe cordifolia*, soft pink mallow-flowers of *Lavatera*

The entrance to the first rose garden showing the long central walk, interrupted by fountain and pool, guarded by four clipped Irish Yews. The Rose 'Raubritter' in glowing pink acts as an off-centre focal point, overhanging the pool. Masses of Lady's Mantle (*Alchemilla mollis*) and the grey *Stachys byzantina* (*S. olympica*) or Lamb's Ears, soften the brick edging, with hardy pinks and other low plants tucked in here and there.

cashmiriana, and waving cream plumes of *Aruncus dioicus*, at one time known as *Spiraea aruncus*. In a kind season *Veratrum nigrum* throws up its tall spikes of chocolate stars.

Waving gently in the breeze are clumps of variegated grass, *Phalaris arundinacea* 'Picta', the grey of *Helictotrichon sempervirens*, and tall, rustling *Miscanthus*. At one corner the Cardoon, *Cynara cardunculus*, dominates everything — huge, silvery, sculptured leaves and gigantic violet-blue thistles higher than one's head, likewise the pale yellow Scabious-relative *Cephalaria gigantea* (synonym *C. tatarica*) and *Macleaya microcarpa* 'Coral Plume' with its superb leaves. It is with these tall plants that the stronger colours are grouped so that, at whichever end you start, the eye first is caught by sharp tints, the better to appreciate the cool hues beyond. They include orange-red *Phygelius capensis coccineus*, double orange Day Lilies, the stalwart yellow heads of *Centaurea macrocephala* and certain kniphofias.

The other central path, crossing the flower borders, has box hedges and several substantial wooden arches; the eye travels each way to handsome, traditional wooden seats, painted white and standing against the far walls, one embowered in Rose 'Constance Spry'. The arches are covered with old rambler roses raised in the early years of the nineteenth century: 'Blush Boursault', 'Princesse Louise' and 'Adélaïde d'Orléans'.

At some time in June, according to the season, the roses start to flower, flooding the garden with fragrance on warm days. And what a feast there is. *Rosa gallica* itself, the great-grandparent of all the European race is there, a suckering single pink rose which reached me from the Honourable Robert James of Richmond, Yorkshire; he had treasured it for many years having received it from Miss Willmott. It is a native of the south of France and farther east. Long before history, in the mists of time, it became hybridized, we believe, with *Rosa phoenicia*, the result being the Damask Rose, *R* × *damascena*. Whether it was called Damask because of its supposed origin in or near Damascus or because its petals were rich and "damascened" I cannot say. The plant we grow today is called *R.* × *damascena* 'Trigintipetala' having thirty or so petals. Hundreds of acres of it are grown in the Kazanlik district of Bulgaria for the extraction of rose water and the almost priceless Attar. This industry is also carried on in India, Iran, Saudi Arabia and elsewhere. The loosely formed flowers are light pink but long, long ago a sport occurred in which some of the petals were wholly or partly white. This sport has always been known as the York and Lancaster Rose.

A large-flowered semi-double sport of *R. gallica* is known as Officinalis which, legend has it, was brought to northern Europe by the Crusaders. Its large flowers have the valuable propensity of retaining their fragrance when dried or made into conserves; thus was formed an industry around Provins in France and at Mitcham in Surrey. It is therefore sometimes called the Rose of Provins and was also dubbed the Red Rose of Lancaster. Its striped sport is Rosa Mundi (*R.g.* 'Versicolor') − often incorrectly called 'York and Lancaster' − in which the petals of light crimson are striped and spotted with blush-white.

All of these roses flower only at midsummer, but *R. gallica* also allied itself, it is surmised, with another species of southern Europe, *R. moschata*, the Musk Rose. It is not known whether this species is truly a wild rose; the plant we grow today is a tall lax shrub which we train on a wall, and it produces intensely fragrant flowers, single, of creamy white and borne in large clusters, from late summer onwards. A double form was called The Coroneola by Parkinson in 1629. *R. moschata* and *R. phoenicia* belong to the same subsection of the genus in which the scent emanates from the stamens, not from the petals. The late flowering of the Musk Rose hybridized with *R. gallica* produced the Autumn Damask which for the gardens of ancient time was a priceless attribute. In fact it is said that the Emperor Nero had plants grown in the warm climate of Alexandria expressly for the importation of flowers for winter feasts in Rome. It is still in cultivation and is a light pink. Both of the Damask roses, and many of their derivatives, have very slender heps, unlike the rounded ones of *R. gallica*.

Yet another of the pre-history ancestral roses is the White Rose of York, *R.* 'Alba Semi-plena' which is believed to be a hybrid between *R. gallica* and a white form of *R. canina*, the Dog Brier, and probably originated in the Middle East. Whereas *R. gallica* and the two Damask roses have many small bristles and prickles, the White Rose inherits only the few large prickles of the Dog Brier, together with its rather greyish leaves. As a

Looking back to the entrance door on page 17 in high summer. The mixed borders focus upon the pool with Rose 'Raubritter' and the sentinel yews. Lady's Mantle is repeated at this end with the plum-crimson of *Penstemon* 'Garnet'; both have long flowering periods. Pinks, Clove Carnations and a big dark green hummock of Thrift (*Armeria maritima* 'Laucheana' for spring display) spill over the brick edges. At intervals are standards of *Hibiscus syriacus* 'Blue Bird', 'Woodbridge' and 'Ardens' for flowering in late summer. They stand opposite the wooden panels of rambling roses, early 'Goldfinch' and later 'Purpurtraum'. The cool pale lilac of *Erigeron* 'Quakeress' meets clumps of *Lilium regale*. Solid groups of light green foliage of pale yellow *Crocosmia* and silvery *Perovskia* 'Blue Spire' break the colour with promise of future flowers.

---

group the old White Roses (some are pink) have a freshness of colour and scent unequalled.

In gardens, over the centuries, these groups of roses were hybridized by insects and became blurred in their characteristics. The great triumph came probably from Holland at some time prior to 1620, when what is known as R. × *centifolia* was distributed. This is called the Hundred-leafed (petalled) Rose or Cabbage Rose, and has been the principal rose depicted by artists in pictures and designs ever since. Its great, nodding, deep-centred flowers almost seem to exude their rich fragrance.

Yet further development occurred. This wondrous rose developed around the turn of the seventeenth century a form whose stalk and calyx are best described as "mossy". The Moss Rose became a great favourite in later years, particularly with the Victorians. The original was pink but 'Shailer's White Moss' is a sport which occurred in 1790. At Mottisfont it sometimes produces a normal pink flower. The "moss" is soft and sticky to the touch. Strangely, the Autumn Damask also produced a mossy sport, in 1835, with white flowers, but the flowers are not shapely though very sweet, and the "moss" is harsh and prickly to the touch. Our plants at Mottisfont often give the pink non-mossy flowers of the Autumn Damask. The fact that, like its parent, the Perpetual White Damask Moss continued to flower into the autumn, made it doubly valuable to growers, though its flowers are a long way behind those of the Centifolia (or Common) Moss in beauty.

A contrast of shape and colour from Rose 'Constance Spry' and pale yellow aquilegias. The rose is trained on a wall, the aquilegias or columbines seed themselves in a variety of soft colours derived from several species, natives of North America. The yellow is contributed by *A. chrysantha* and all colours of seedsmen's modern strain inherit the long spurs. Both names, Aquilegia and Columbine, derive from birds, eagle and dove respectively, because if looked at closely each flower resembles a cluster of birds, with long necks. Shorter necks are seen in the older columbines or "Granny's Bonnets", but these lack the delicacy of colours. All kinds are comparatively short-lived and should be allowed to seed themselves, when some surprising and lively combinations of colours will ensue.

Striving after further variety, nurserymen — mainly in France but later also in England — saved seeds from all these roses, open-pollinated before the art of hybridization was understood. Literally thousands of seedlings were raised and a general *mélange* ensued. Thus the Gallicas brought their compact upright growth, flat formal flowers of pink, purple and maroon; the Summer Damasks their intense fragrance, loose pink blooms and lanky growth; the Autumn Damasks their small pink flowers and recurrent flowering habit and rich fragrance; the White Roses their great prickly stems and purity of colour and scent; the Cabbage Roses their arching growth, large leaves and globular flowers of intense sweetness and with them all the two Moss Roses mingled. It is often difficult to assign the later derivatives definitely to one group or another.

In addition to this mainstream of roses raised deliberately from seed — raisers were always hoping, no doubt, for bigger and brighter blooms — there are a few others of separate lineage such as 'Dupontii' of 1817, a possible hybrid of the Musk and the Damask Rose. Then there is the rose we grow as 'Empress Joséphine'; the story goes that it was brought to England by the *émigrés*, but there is no record in the old French books of a variety of this Frankfurt Rose being named after the Empress. We are also rather in the dark about the origin of the Scarlet Four Seasons often called the Portland Rose. Truly in flower from midsummer until the autumn if the spent flowers are promptly removed, it is reputedly a hybrid between *R. gallica* and the Autumn Damask. Its name becomes this low suckering plant for it is certainly the brightest red of all these old roses.

20

Yet another delicious old rose is 'Stanwell Perpetual', believed to be a hybrid between the Autumn Damask and the Scotch Brier.

There seem to me to be some essentials in catering for a garden of these old French roses. One is the need for plenty of white to offset the predominance of pinks and mauves; this can be partly assured by repeated groups of the best white varieties, those of York and also the Damasks 'Madame Hardy' and 'Madame Zoetmans' but also by clumps of White Sweet Rocket (*Hesperis matronalis*), white foxgloves, *Campanula alliariifolia* and lavender-blue and white *Campanula persicifolia*. Another need is for more lavender-blue, such as *Salvia haematodes* (sometimes considered to be a variety of *S. pratensis*), and pale yellow from the Foxglove *Digitalis grandiflora* and *Phlomis russeliana*. Many such pale tints of blue, yellows, white and pale pink are to be found in the Long-spur hybrids of columbines or aquilegias which provide a delicacy of line unequalled by other flowers.

Slightly alien to all the old European stalwarts listed above is a bed devoted to hybrids of the China Rose, *Rosa chinensis*. These all stem from the four original hybrids mentioned earlier. Among them is the original 'Parsons's Pink' which was depicted on Chinese silks over 1000 years ago. Others reveal some of the coppery or yellowish tints inherent in these hybrids. They all flower continuously until the autumn. I find it a most absorbing thought that the small race of roses treasured by the ancient Chinese united with our equally old European hybrids to act as parents to all the roses grown today, the outcome of thousands of years of culture.

The first hybrids of any importance to crop up from the China roses were yellowish – the old Noisette and Tea climbers. They were the most spectacular advance in roses; 'Lamarque', 'Desprez à fleur jaune', 'Céline Forestier', 'Gloire de Dijon' and 'Alister Stella Gray', raised between 1830 and 1894, are still in the forefront of the most fragrant and continuously flowering roses today. Thus did the old Chinese Tea Rose, 'Parks's Yellow', serve us.

Contemporaneous, almost, with the above yellow climbers was the race of Bourbon roses, derived from another of the ancient, pink Chinese hybrids; they retained all the old European colours but added the stronger repeat-flowering habit and smoother leaves. They are small and large bushes, approaching climbers. There are such gems as 'Reine Victoria' and its pale sport 'Madame Pierre Oger', never equalled for the charm of their circular blooms, and the camellia-like white 'Boule de Neige'. Much taller is 'Honorine de Brabant' with globular pale pink blooms striped with lilac. Following on are the Hybrid Perpetuals with richer colours and larger blooms, often giving a good second crop, and their vigour is usually considerable.

So there is the picture, however inadequate, of the first Old Rose Garden, the beauty of which is best savoured on a midsummer day.

‘WILLIAMS’ DOUBLE YELLOW’

The Scots Brier hybrid rose ‘Williams’ Double Yellow’, raised from seeds of *R. foetida*, the so-called Austrian Brier, is of the same parentage as *R.* x *harisonii* but lacks the stamens of the latter, their place being taken by a bunch of palest green stigmata. The brilliant yellow of the petals and the heavy aroma are the same, likewise the early crop of flowers. ‘Williams’ Double Yellow’ is also known as the Old Double Yellow Scots Rose, and, like Harison’s, (see page 13), needs the minimum of pruning, a mere thinning out of old twiggy wood immediately after flowering. Both roses spread underground by their own suckering roots, but their prickly intrusiveness can be forgiven for the sake of their brilliant blooms. It has to be admitted that the American Harison’s Yellow has an advantage over Williams’ in that the latter’s flowers stay on the bush when faded and sere; on the other hand Williams’ makes a more bushy plant. It is seen here with an underplanting of Thrift, a richly coloured form of *Armeria maritima* called ‘Laucheana’; both the rose and the Thrift are ardent sun-lovers and thrive in poor soils.

22

EARLY BOLD FOLIAGE

A photograph taken in May, revealing the value of good foliage before flowers appear. It owes much to the silvery filigree of the Cardoon (*Cynara cardunculus*) leaves in the foreground grouped against a mound of tiny leaves of the Giant Catmint (*Nepeta gigantea*). Behind these are the vertical sword-leaves of *Iris* 'Ochraurea' in blue-green, backed by arching bright green leaves of Day Lilies. Just beyond are the broad, pleated blades of *Veratrum nigrum*, while to the right is a big clump of the giant pale yellow Scabious, *Cephalaria gigantea*. Beyond, in a sea of greyish green from grasses and geraniums, the standard *Hibiscus syriacus* stand up starkly. They are always chary about braving the fickle English spring with too-early growth. The sentinel Irish Yews have not yet been given their restraining strings to correct their waywardness after the winter's gales.

THE MIXED BORDERS IN EARLY SUMMER

A view of the mixed borders in early summer. Here the old crimson peony 'Adolphe Rousseau' is dominant. In the immediate foreground is the larger Catmint, *Nepeta gigantea*, while beyond the peonies is a drift of the smaller Catmint, *Nepeta x faassenii*, often labelled *N. mussinii* which is in reality an inferior plant. It is important to plant catmints in warm spring weather; they do not take kindly to autumn planting; if trimmed over after the first flush of bloom is past they will give more subsequent crops. The subdued purplish colouring on the farther border is the young foliage of the purple-leafed Sage, *Salvia officinalis* 'Purpurascens' which will burst into violet-blue flowers later. Like the Catmint, it is best planted in spring, witness the old saying: 'plant sage in May and it will grow all day'. A group of the pale lilac *Erigeron* 'Quakeress' is next, with Lamb's Ears or *Stachys byzantina* (*S. olympica*, *S. lanata*) nearer to the path in soft grey. At the end of the border is a little-known Knotweed, *Polygonum alpinum*, in creamy white, a pretty lacy effect. Two of the standard *Hibiscus syriacus* are in their young, pale-leafed stage.

'GLOIRE DES MOUSSEUX' (*above*)

The sturdy form of an old Moss Rose, 'Gloire des Mousseux' of 1852, with the bed of China Rose hybrids in the background. The Moss rose is a superlative example of the quality and perfection that these old roses can attain. In 'Gloire des Mousseux' we have superior vigorous growth, light green leaves and mossy buds, opening into large, full blooms, expanding well and reflexing, of clear bright pink, fading to paler tones. They are long-lasting and rich in fragrance. The plants will achieve 5ft (1.5m) in height and nearly as much in width, and flower profusely at midsummer. In contrast is the China Rose, 'Mutabilis', laden with coppery, single blossoms. It opens chamois-yellow from flame buds and turns to pink and then to crimson, at all times with a coppery undertone, blending with the tinted leaves. This is a most valuable rose, flowering non-stop until autumn. It should be given a sheltered, sunny position, because it is apt to suffer in hard winters. Single hybrid pinks furnish the front of the bed with tones of pink in early midsummer, coupled with clumps of grey foliage for the rest of the season.

'ADELAIDE D'ORLEANS' (*opposite*)

This originated in France in 1826 (presumably from open-pollinated seed, since hybridizing was not then understood) and suggests *R. sempervirens* as a possible parent. Of extreme grace, the lax clusters *hang down*. It would not reveal its beauty if trained on a wall, so it is best over an arch or a tree. (This arch is made from stripped sweet chestnut, with its bases soaked in preservative.)

There is one overpowering crop of blossom with the delicate scent of primroses. Dead-heading is not necessary and little pruning is required — just the removal of old branches and the tying back of new ones.

26

'Cerise Bouquet' (*above*)

'Cerise Bouquet' is a modern hybrid, combining the great vigour of *Rosa multibracteata* with the sumptuousness of the Hybrid Tea rose 'Crimson Glory'. The long arching sprays are exceedingly prickly and bear the multitude of bracts that one would expect from the first parent. From the second parent is inherited the rich colour and ability to produce a good late summer crop. In the foreground is a small plant of Sweet Brier. Both of these roses were of temporary planting and were removed to make room for the corner entrance in to the Second Garden.

Opposite is a hybrid peony with the Giant Catmint and *Achillea* 'Flowers of Sulphur'. There are many of these hybrid achilleas in gardens today, being intercrosses between the old garden plants 'Clypeolata' and x *taygetea*. The latter's influence brings the softer yellows. They are all good perennials if planted in spring and their flat-topped flower heads give a distinctive line to the border. All peonies are best planted in early autumn.

'SISSINGHURST CASTLE' (*above*)

It is *Rosa gallica* (see page 57) which provides the sumptuous dark velvety crimsons, maroons and purples of the old roses. 'Sissinghurst Castle' is so named because it was growing wild at Sissinghurst when Harold Nicolson and Vita Sackville-West bought the property. I have seen it also in a Somerset garden, without a name. The suggested name 'Rose des Maures' has no foundation. Like other Gallicas, if grown on its own roots it runs about like couch-grass. With all these roses of subdued colouring it needs a white companion, here provided by white foxgloves (*Digitalis purpurea* 'Alba') which break the hummocks of the shrubs with their tapering spires. They are biennial, but sow themselves freely – sometimes too freely! In the spring it is wise to examine each strong-growing seedling and discard those which have a greyish or purplish reverse to the leaves – specially on the main vein and stalk; these will produce the ordinary purplish-pink flowers and will hybridize with the white. We do our best to keep to white only. But in the foreground are several spikes of the shorter growing *Digitalis grandiflora*, which used to be called *D. ambigua*. Its soft creamy yellow flowers are produced on a perennial plant, but for all that it also seeds itself. Tidy gardeners, beware: always leave a few foxglove stems to mature and produce seeds. They give endless pleasure, to my eyes, in stature as well as in colour.

(*Opposite*) Irises and peonies give us the first awakening to summer colour in our gardens. They are both ardent sun-lovers. In the picture is one of the many rich pink peonies of the Lactiflora group together with the old Bearded Iris 'Flavescens'; both were in Mrs Gilbert Russell's borders when the Trust assumed control of the garden. We like to keep them there. Today the iris-specialists would not give more than a passing glance to the iris, but it has two assets: it flowers very freely early in the season and its rhizomes are compact, forming a dense clump of leaves which defy weeds. And of course the pale creamy yellow colouring, delicately veined on the haft with light brown, blends with anything.

30

THE MIXED BORDERS IN MIDSUMMER

A photograph taken rather later than the picture on pages 24–5, looking up the mixed borders from the entrance to the rose garden. Lady's Mantle (*Alchemilla mollis*) and *Sisyrinchium striatum* are at their best; the spring-flowering Alpine phloxes and thrifts are over. Pinks and Lamb's Ears, *Stachys byzantina*, are also at their best and the great plumes of *Aruncus dioicus* (*A. sylvester*), the giant Goat's Beard, wave between the sentinel yews which guard the central pool.

APPROACH TO THE CENTRAL POOL

Moving up the path, the rose 'Raubritter' comes into focus and the eye can travel along the second length of borders to the archway in the wall, revealing a portion of the delights of the Second Rose Garden.

The Irish Yews are trimmed and tied in late summer. The best time to clip the short Box hedges is in May; soon after, fresh greenery appears to remain in good colour for the rest of the year. There is, however, such pressure of work in May that the clipping does not all get done to time. August is also a good time to clip garden hedges, but they do not always respond with new short growth until the following spring.

'COMPLICATA' (*above*)

It is the white centre and yellow stamens which give the rose 'Complicata' its brilliance, enhancing the already vivid clear pink. It is sometimes called *R. gallica* 'Complicata', but, while the Gallica rose is almost certainly in its parentage, it is a rose of unknown origin. Old, flowering wood should be cleared away after flowering and all the long new shoots of the summer need making secure by ties before the spring. But it will make a great mound on its own with little pruning, and flowers very freely every year.

(*Opposite*) This 'Complicata' has used its great vigour to climb into an apple tree, first encouraged by being tied to a pole. Roses for growing into trees should be planted well away from the trunk of the tree. The shoots may reach 8ft (2.4m) or more in a season, the following summer to break into short shoots from every leaf-eye, each bearing a cluster of very large single blooms. Early in the season there are few more spectacular roses to be found. Here it has for companions white foxgloves and the warm violet-blue of *Campanula persicifolia*. This is the peach-leafed Bellflower; it is an old garden favourite known since 1596, a native of Europe, North Africa and Asia. It is a spreader at the root and also seeds itself, white forms often occurring.

35

THE CENTRAL POOL IN MIDSUMMER

The centre of the garden on a brilliant midsummer morning. The severity of the hedges and topiary are contrasted by the elegant lines of the garden seats, metal copies of an eighteenth-century design. All these lines and that of the coping round the pool are firm and formal. In contrast are Nature's flowing lines and informal exuberance of rose 'Raubritter', the cream feathers of Goat's Beard, *Aruncus dioicus*, and in the foreground the purple-leafed culinary Sage, *Salvia officinalis* 'Purpurascens'. The latter is best grown from cuttings struck in September in the open ground and transferred to permanent quarters in early May. The Goat's Beard has male and female flowers on separate plants. The male dies off, brown, a few weeks after flowering but is the more plumose and luxuriant in flower. The female produces greenish, drooping panicles of seeds, which will germinate freely – to either sex – in moist ground. Though closely related to herbaceous spiraeas (*Ulmaria*) which thrive best in moist soils, the *Aruncus* is not so dependent on moisture.

Here we are approaching the pool and 'Raubritter' rose from the far end, with the rich colour of *Stachys macrantha* (18in/45cm) in the foreground, backed by the delicate tint of *Erigeron* 'Quakeress'. They are both easily grown plants, suitable for division in spring and may be relied upon to give a good display in late June. The sentinel Irish Yews have to be kept in shape not only by clipping but by string; in the picture after a gale one string had broken and thus the tree has a peculiar outline.

'Raubritter'

Wilhelm Kordes produced this variety in Germany in 1936. He had tried many species in an endeavour to get very hardy roses for cold central Europe. This is a hybrid between the old garden rose 'Macrantha', itself very hardy, and 'Solarium', a vermilion-red rambler which had been raised in 1925. Few would have expected the result.

The growth of the rose is lax, but it can be trained over large shrubs or small trees to 15ft (4.5m) and will grow and flower in semi-shade. At Mottisfont it is in full sun, billowing over the side of a pool at the centre of the old rose garden. It is the only rose I know which could be controlled to the shape that I needed for this position.

Each flower lasts a week, so there is a long flowering period at the height of the rose season. There is little scent, but it is a graceful rose in bloom and the small, globular flowers (1½in/4cm diameter) have great charm.

Very little attention is needed. Dead heads should be removed and very old branches reduced or cut out immediately after flowering, which will encourage new growth during the later summer and provide maximum strong wood for flowering the following year. The flower stalks can suffer attacks of mildew sometimes, but this is of little account. It is a very weather-resistant rose.

'CONSTANCE SPRY' (*above and opposite*)

Raised by David Austin, Wolverhampton, in 1961, this rose is a hybrid between an old Gallica Rose, 'Belle Isis', and a floribunda, 'Dainty Maid'. Even with wild imagination, David Austin could not have conjured up anything so beautiful from its parents. The flower harks back to the most sumptuous of old roses and has the rare fragrance of myrrh, known in only two roses of earlier origin, neither of which is in the parentage. But if a new colour could crop up in the 1920s, why not a new scent in the 1960s?

The lax growth is unmanageable as a bush; it is therefore best on a wall or support. It covers the wall behind the elegant white seat in the picture opposite; this is a good focal point, drawing the eye to the wonderful rose that acts as its backcloth. Growths that have flowered should be shortened, old wood removed and new growths tied back in winter.

'OEILLET PARFAIT'

The walks that follow the lines of the walls surround the four quarters of the garden and are hedged with box. This long walk is on the north side of the garden and the wall border is filled with Hybrid Perpetuals, while climbers cover the wall. The ancient Damask hybrid rose 'Oeillet Parfait' is posing for the camera; note the fresh green leaves, the flowers densely filled with petals, reflexing into almost a ball as they expand and release their rich scent. It was raised in France in 1841. It is important to remember that there is a striped Gallica Rose of the same name.

42

'HIPPOLYTE'

This photograph shows one of the beds fronting onto a lawn. Once again white foxgloves come into their own in statuesque quality in contrast to the dark purplish colour of rose 'Hippolyte'. This is a Gallica hybrid for which we have no date. Strangely it is almost prickle-less and in this way as in the shape and colour of the flowers Gallica ancestry is indicated. Reaching 5 or 6ft (1.5 or 1.8m) in height it is of graceful habit, bearing beautiful little flat flowers like rosettes, smooth petalled, reflexing into a ball, with 'button' eyes. An occasional cerise petal, or one of dove-grey, light the many others which are generally of soft rosy violet. The "button" eye is a character peculiar to the very full-petalled old roses; the centres, composed of stamens turned into petals are packed so tightly into the empty receptacle in the heart of the flower that they cannot unfold and remain in an incurved cluster, shaped like a button. There is a broad edging of seed-raised Highland Hybrid pinks of various colours all of which, from white to dark pink, variously marked, blend well with the roses and contribute their own rich fragrance.

43

'ROSE-MARIE VIAUD'

One of the small lawns freely decorated with roses and their companions. In the foreground, in one of the mixed borders, is a clump of the purple-leafed Sage, again in full flower. Then the grassy leaves of pale yellow Montbretias (*Crocosmia*). The pure white is of the double-flowered Dropwort, *Filipendula vulgaris* 'Plena' (*F. hexapetala* 'Plena'). Its beautiful ferny leaves make a dense mass over the ground and it is easy to divide and establish. The single-flowered type is a native of our chalk downs. Next to it is a dark crimson Scabious, *Knautia macedonica*. It is important to get the dark coloured form; it varies to a disappointing pink tint. One often sees this plant staked up like a besom broom, but it is much better to encourage it to flop on the ground, sending up batch after batch of dark pin-cushion flowers. These all form a setting to another of the wooden panels at the back of the border, devoted to rose 'Rose-Marie Viaud', a Multiflora rambler in soft lilac-pink. It was named in 1924, a seedling from the better known 'Veilchenblau', the so-called 'blue rambler' (see page 62). Though stronger growing and virtually thornless, 'Rose-Marie Viaud' lacks scent.

44

'FERDINAND PICHARD'

There is a small group of Bourbon roses which show a marked affinity to one another. 'Commandant Beaurepaire' was raised in France in 1879 and is a big sprawling bush with one crop of cupped pink flowers splashed and striped with rose-madder, crimson and purple. 'Honorine de Brabant' bears some resemblance, but is more vigorous in growth with blush flowers striped and spotted with mauve. In 1909 'Variegata di Bologna' was raised in Italy. It is a strong climber with almost white, globular flowers striped with vivid crimson-purple. The above photograph is of 'Ferdinand Pichard' raised in France as late as 1921. It is a good upright shrub with a plentiful crop of midsummer flowers, and like 'Honorine de Brabant' is seldom without flowers until the autumn. What unites these four roses is their foliage − smooth, dark green, with the terminal leaflet drawn out to a fine point. 'Ferdinand Pichard' well repays frequent dead-heading and feeding and should be thinned and reduced in winter.

'GLOIRE DE DIJON'

For many years after its appearance in 1853 'Gloire de Dijon' was the most popular, hardy and prolific of the yellowish climbers. It has remained in the lists ever since, a wonderful plant with good foliage and a richness of scent unsurpassed — so long, that is, as it is grown and nurtured well, in good soil. Its parents were the famous 'Souvenir de la Malmaison' of 1843 or earlier, and a Tea Rose. It is not generally realized that gardeners were blessed with several of these yellowish Tea-Noisettes with large scented flowers, long before other colours appeared among climbers. 'Desprez à fleur jaune', 1830 (see page 124), 'Céline Forestier', 1842, preceded 'Gloire de Dijon'; 'Maréchal Niel' and 'Alister Stella Gray' followed it. They are all unique and unbeatable in their way, even now. 'Gloire' is apt to be ''leggy'' but this slight defect can be alleviated when it is growing between shrubs on a wall. It is not suitable for pillars or arches. Thinning out old twiggy growth in January, to encourage those coppery-leafed, new basal shoots, is all that is required.

Sisyrinchium striatum

A bee's eye view of *Sisyrinchium striatum*. It is a native of Chile and was first introduced to our gardens as long ago as 1788. It is a perennial but old clumps are apt to die after prolific flowering. However it produces abundant seedlings, without variation. It is not much use to commuters — except at weekends — because the flowers close in the afternoon. On a June morning it gives an uplift to any stodgy border with its vertical line and clear pale tint.

'SPONG'

On pages 54–5 we see one of the most famous of sports of *R.* x *centifolia*, 'De Meaux'. This is a later sport, 'Spong', which originated in 1805, probably in England. It will reach 4ft (1.2m), bears the typically rounded leaves of its parent and neat flowers about twice the size of 'De Meaux' with the same good fragrance. Its failing is that the petals are apt to stay on the bush after fading. Prune after flowering. It is a charmer for a small garden.

(*Opposite*) Here is early morning light on the central path between the mixed borders, with *Sisyrinchium striatum* in evidence. In the foreground are seedling pinks and a few flowers of *Rosa stellata mirifica*. This is a little-known variety from the Sacramento Mountains in New Mexico, U.S.A., where it makes an impenetrable mass of suckering stems up to about 3ft (90cm), acres in extent. It is quite hardy and easy to grow. Both *R. stellata* itself and its more easily grown variety often have only three leaflets to each leaf; their resemblance to those of a gooseberry has confounded many a keen gardener. The flowers are silky, much like those of a *Cistus*. Beyond the rose is our old friend Lady's Mantle and the rose 'Raubritter' by the pool can be seen in the distance. Is there anything so refreshing as a garden seen soon after sunrise?

'SURPASSE TOUT' (*above and opposite*)

We have no date, unfortunately, for this excellent Gallica Rose called appropriately 'Surpasse Tout'. It makes a splendid bush and is of pure Gallica derivation judging by the foliage, bud, shape of flower and absence of large prickles. It is, with 'Assemblage des Beautés', dating from 1790, among the most brilliant of light crimsons, passing to deep cerise pink with a delicate veining of a darker shade. It was as bright a tone of red as was attainable before the advent of crimson derived from the China rose. The petals in the flower depicted are what we call 'quartered' — that is arranged into radial sections, and often have a marked button eye.

Hybrid pinks, as a foreground to 'Surpasse Tout', which is as full of fragrance as of petals. As with all Gallica roses, remove old flowered branches immediately after flowering and reduce the resulting new shoots to the general outline of the bush in winter.

'Empress Joséphine'

Here is the rose we know as 'Empress Joséphine', though there is no record in any old French book of a rose named after Napoleon's first wife, who inspired Redouté to such heights of artistry. It has one serious defect — it is only slightly scented. But think of the assets: almost prickle-less, good pleated foliage, abundance of full, gracious flowers, appearing later than most, and a glorious colour. It is reputed to have been brought over to England by the *émigrés* during the French Revolution. At all events, though without much scent, it has magnificence and gives annually great delight. Pruning as for any Gallica rose. It will reach 3–4ft (0.9–1.2m).

'PRÉSIDENT DE SÈZE'

'Président de Sèze' is a true Gallica with excellent bushy, arching growth up to 4–5ft (1.2–1.5m) high and wide, good foliage and few prickles. It is an ancient variety raised prior to 1836; the same rose is also grown, erroneously, as 'Jenny Duval'. The big blooms are very full of petals and are often quartered and with button eyes. The colours move from dark magenta-crimson in the centre of a half-open flower paling to lilac-white round the edges. It is at all times, even when the whole flower has faded to pale lilac, a rich and striking bloom. As a contrast in the sea of blooms at midsummer are the tall pale heliotrope or lavender-blue spikes of *Salvia haematodes*, a native of Greece and a beautiful addition to our rose garden in line and colour. It is not always long-lived but is easily raised from seed. Again as a contrast behind them are the bushes of *R. x alba* 'Maxima', the Jacobite Rose, or Great Double White, a sport of the semi-double White Rose of York. This brings considerable height, up to 6ft (1.8m) or more, leaden green leaves and comparatively few large prickles on the pale green stalwart stems. Its origin is lost.

'DE MEAUX' AND 'ZIGEUNERKNABE'

Throughout its long life in European gardens — from late in the seventeenth century — *Rosa* x *centifolia* has been prodigal with sports, such as the beautiful Moss rose and the miniature 'De Meaux', here pictured with 'Zigeunerknabe'. 'De Meaux' appeared prior to 1799. The plants depicted were several years old but may achieve 3–4ft (0.9–1.2m) being at all times bushy but graceful as the branches lean outwards with the weight of the many small rounded leaves and flowers, each one a perfect rosette. An albino, white with pink centre, is 'White de Meaux'. Behind 'De Meaux' are young plants of 'Zigeunerknabe' or 'Gipsy Boy', sometimes classed as a Bourbon rose, but with little justification. Although not raised until 1909 and a modern rose in many ways, it assorts well with the Old Roses making very large, wide bushes smothered in its deeply coloured, plum-crimson flowers. Prune after flowering for all these roses.

The Foxgloves in the foreground are the pale yellow perennial *Digitalis grandiflora* from Greece, with masses of the white native behind interspersed with white *Campanula persicifolia*. This picture changes from year to year, as the roses grow and according to how many foxgloves are allowed to appear.

'CARDINAL DE RICHELIEU'

One of the richest coloured Gallica hybrid roses is 'Cardinal de Richelieu' named after the famous seventeenth-century prelate and statesman. It probably owes some of its being to the China Rose, on account of its smooth stems and leaves. Be this as it may, the flower is unequalled in its depth of velvety grape-purple on the front of the petals, backed by lilac pink. This results in the button-eye being of light colour, accentuated by the almost white centre. It makes a fine bush, laden with flowers. Prune away weak wood after flowering and reduce lanky shoots in February.

R. gallica

The meek little rose is the great-grandparent of all the old European roses, *R. gallica* itself. It is a low bush, freely suckering and making dense thickets about 2ft (60cm) high. The flowers are very appealing, though fleeting, and give little promise of the stalwart bushes that actually accrued from it, nor the glorious velvety dark mauves and purples that were to develop in the hands of the fanciers of the late eighteenth and nineteenth centuries. It seems almost impossible. The small, neat folded leaves are another noted character of the French rose, likewise its few prickles. In common with most single roses it produces a good crop of rounded, red heps. What more suitable background could be devised than the slender poise of white foxgloves?

'MADAME HARDY' (*above*)

The incomparable 'Madame Hardy', which made her entry in 1832, will always be in our gardens. The photograph reinforces the selection of the title of "shrub roses" for these stalwarts of the nineteenth century. When my first list of these old roses for sale was issued in the early 1950s I chose *The Old Shrub Roses* for its title; this was to indicate that the plants were completely different from the innumerable bush roses — the Hybrid Teas and the Floribundas — of popular esteem. And what a display the shrub roses make, as this book will demonstrate to the unconvinced. 'Madame Hardy' has all the assets — superlative blooms, flatly and fully double, quartered, with button eyes and a green pointel in the centre and an unforgettable, sweet scent. All this on a fine big shrub with good foliage. Prune after flowering and reduce long shoots in winter.

(*Opposite*) The single flowered pinks which occur in so many of these photographs — simply because we use them all round the beds which edge the lawns — are known as Highland Hybrids. This is because at one time a number were named from a Scottish garden. I am perfectly content with raising them from seeds. They vary from white through blush and all tones of pink to light crimson, many having a ring of dark red around the centre. They are not always long-lived but are easy to strike from cuttings in September in the open ground if one wants to preserve a specially beautiful seedling. They flower when the Old Roses are first coming into bloom. Here is a once-flowering Bourbon rose of immense vigour, 'Blairii Number 2' (see pages 78 and 79), trained up an old apple tree and smothering it with bloom.

58

Polygonum alpinum

Knotweeds, as they are called in an uncomplimentary way, apply to all species of *Polygonum*, some of which are truly ineradicable weeds. *P. alpinum* is a small-growing charmer for early summer, spreading slowly by underground roots and never failing in its flowering. It is a native of parts of Europe and has been grown in our gardens for nearly 200 years and yet is seldom seen. Spearing through it is another European native, *Gladiolus communis byzantinus*. It is quite hardy in Britain, spreads freely by seeds or division of the small brown corms and annually delights me with its gorgeous, Byzantine richness of colouring, containing crimson, maroon, pink, purple and coppery-brown; there are three cream stripes on the lowest segments. It is almost indescribable.

'Madame Delaroche-Lambert'

'Madame Delaroche-Lambert' of 1851 is one of the most sumptuous and richly coloured of Moss roses. It will reach 4–5ft (1.2–1.5m) and, after the midsummer flush of bloom, continually produces odd, lovely blooms. From this it may be deduced that it is a hybrid of the Perpetual Damask Moss. The young foliage and the moss on the stems are brownish, but the buds are copiously swathed in green moss, and have elegant, long, foliaceous sepals, containing buds of dark colouring. The flowers open fully, revealing muddled centres. It has a good scent and prompt dead-heading will encourage the later flower crops. As a companion this group of roses has the invaluable *Campanula alliariifolia*, just coming into full bloom. The clumps of good rounded leaves from a long-lived rootstock give rise regularly to the sprays of ivory white bells. It is native to the Caucasus and Asia Minor and was first recorded in 1803 — but how many gardeners grow it?

'VEILCHENBLAU' AND 'SNOWDRIFT' (*above*)

The garden being more or less square, we had walls of all aspects to cover. Those catching the most sun play host to the more tender Tea and Noisette roses; the north-facing wall was given some very hardy ramblers. The so-called "Blue Rambler", 'Veilchenblau' (violet-blue), and 'Snowdrift' grow together on this wall and never disappoint us, especially because both are sweetly scented. 'Veilchenblau' was raised in Germany in 1901, the result of crossing the old 'Crimson Rambler' with 'Erinnerung an Brod', a Hybrid Perpetual rose. It is unique among the several purplish ramblers since, after opening from crimson-purple buds, the flowers gradually fade to a lilac-grey, each one having a small white stripe or two. The scent is rosy-sweet whereas 'Snowdrift', raised four years later, has a scent of fresh green apples inherited from its *R. wichuraiana* parent. These two ramblers make a good pair and require the same pruning. If you have time, remove all the old flowering wood immediately the blooms have faded; if not, as soon as you can, and tie up the young new shoots.

'MADAME ZOETMANS' (*opposite*)

Good old *Saponaria ocymoides*, an engaging, floriferous romper usually grown on rock gardens, is equally at home in any well drained soil. It is a native of the Alps and Pyrenees and loves full sunshine. Its sheaves of pink flowers blend very happily with the Damask rose 'Madame Zoetmans' which owns to a faint blush over her white petals. The petals are many, densely filling the sumptuous flowers and are usually quartered and with button eyes. The growth is short, to about 3ft (90cm), but is inclined to be floppy and repays the support of three or four stout stakes 2ft (60cm) out of the ground connected with horizontals at the top, over which the stems can gracefully hang.

'JOHN HOPPER'

It is fortunate that the modern strains of Long-Spurred aquilegias give such an interesting range of colours; all but the most fiercely red blend or contrast well with the Old Roses. This creamy yellow was self sown and it could not have chosen its companion — the Hybrid Perpetual rose 'John Hopper' — more successfully. The light delicacy of the one is a fine contrast to the heavy richness of the other. 'John Hopper' was introduced in 1862 and remains one of the best and most compact of the Hybrid Perpetuals. It should be dead-headed promptly to encourage an autumn crop, and long shoots should be reduced or tied down to a neighbouring plant.

BOX-EDGED ROSE BORDERS

These box hedges were clipped in early May and have achieved a good coverage of fresh greenery by the end of June. On the right several varieties of *Rosa rugosa*, a Japanese species known as the Ramanas Rose, overhang the hedge. On the left is the blush pink 'Daisy Hill' and the tall-growing 'Tour de Malakoff'. The former is a hybrid of *R.* 'Macrantha' as grown in gardens but instead of Macrantha's single five-petalled flowers it is semi-double. The yellow stamens show up the delicate colouring and it has a pronounced fragrance. Behind it, climbing into an old pear tree, is the Centifolia hybrid 'Tour de Malakoff' of 1856. This is a most remarkable rose for the colours found in its extra large, loosely double blooms. From deep magenta-pink the petals on a hot day develop to a deep parma-violet with flecks and blushes of many intermediate shades, eventually developing into lilac-grey. It is a startling revelation of what a rose can do. It is a sprawling, loose grower and needs support. 'Daisy Hill' is best left on its own to make a low mound. Prune both after flowering, removing all weak twiggy growths.

Crambe maritima (above)

Marked contrast in habit if not in colour. In the foreground are the large branching flower heads of *Crambe maritima*, the culinary Seakale. Apart from its flowers it has the most magnificent of all glaucous-grey leaves, lobed blades, fretted and scrolled, better than any cabbage. Its wonderful shape and colour made it a great favourite of Gertrude Jekyll. Total contrast is found in the erect woolly-grey (not glaucous) stems and flower spikes also swathed in grey wool of Lamb's Ears or *Stachys byzantina* (*S. olympica, S. lanata*). Both plants need sharp drainage and full sun; the first is a native of sand-dunes round the coasts of Britain and both are natives of Europe.

'BOURBON QUEEN' (*opposite*)

'Bourbon Queen' is one of the Bourbon roses that only flowers once, at midsummer. Since 1835 it has endeared itself to gardeners because you may be fairly sure to find it in any garden where Old Roses are grown, often without a name. In French it is 'Rose de l'Ile Bourbon'. It can be kept as a bush by pinching out the long shoots that accrue during the summer, or may be trained up to 8ft (2.4m) or so on supports. The leaves are smooth and broad, leathery and distinctly toothed. The semi-double flowers are cupped, loose and open, displaying to advantage their lilac-pink crinkled petals veined with a darker shade. Here some *Sisyrinchium striatum* have been introduced to create a harmony of soft tints.

66

Moss Roses

Three Moss roses in early morning. In the foreground is 'Mousseline', the small dark pink is 'Little Gem' and the big pink bush is 'Gloire des Mousseux' (see also page 26). 'Mousseline' is also sometimes called 'Alfred de Dalmas' and dates from 1855. It is a dense-growing bush owing some affinity to the Portland roses in its recurrent flowering habit and short moss. 'Little Gem' (1880) and 'Gloire des Mousseux' (1852) flower only the once, but create as good a show as any. The small flowers and leaves of 'Little Gem' are rather outclassed by 'Gloire des Mousseux' which I find the most wonderful in strength of growth and size of flower and general magnificence; the flowers are globular and huge, a clear light pink, the rolled petals fading paler. These last two should be pruned in summer as with all once-flowering roses, but 'Mousseline' should be constantly dead-headed to encourage later flowers, and thinned in winter.

Penstemon '\sc GARNET'

Penstemon 'Garnet' is a wonderful plum-crimson and hardy even in cold winters; though it may die to the ground it will still put up a brave show in summer. It was raised in Germany and originally named 'Andenken an Friedrich Hahn'. Behind it, just opening its flowers, are the blue spikes of *Veronica longifolia*, which is a native of Europe and parts of Asia and has long been grown in our gardens; it is a sound perennial and seldom needs staking. The arch gives a tempting view into the Second Garden, through a curtain of scents from two roses and a Honeysuckle.

'SOUVENIR DU DOCTEUR JAMAIN'

Two very famous old Hybrid Perpetual roses, 'Général Jacqueminot' and 'Charles Lefebvre', were hybridized by François Lacharme in Lyon, France, and the triumphant result was 'Souvenir du Docteur Jamain'. Who the good doctor was is not recorded, but his rose will be forever famous for its intense dark colouring. It is a vigorous grower and is best trained on a north-west wall where the sun will not scorch its velvety texture. No other rose can rival the intense crimson-maroon tint; and fortunately it has an excellent scent and produces later blooms after the first overwhelming crop. For this reason it pays to dead-head it regularly during the summer as well as giving it a thinning in winter, removing all small twiggy growth.

'LEDA' (*above and opposite*)

Here is a unique rose, 'Leda', which originated in England prior to 1832. It is of Damask derivation and has very dark green leaves which make a wonderful backcloth to the pale flowers. But who would think the glistening white flowers could emerge from those tight, dark, red-brown buds? Some flowers are almost entirely white, others carry the tint of the bud on the edges of the petals, earning it the name of 'Painted Damask'. It makes a good, sturdy bush of some 4ft (1.2m) and requires the usual thinning out of all once-flowering roses.

A bush of 'Leda' in full flower. Behind it is 'York and Lancaster' and behind that is 'Oeillet Parfait', both Damask roses. On the right of the path is the maroon-crimson Gallica 'Tuscany', which is very old, so old that no record of its occurrence is to be found. Moreover, it is loosely semi-double, an unsophisticated rose and certainly not a fancier's rose. It seldom achieves more than 3ft (90cm). As mentioned in the introduction, 'York and Lancaster' has flowers white or pink or particoloured. 'Oeillet Parfait', of 1841, has particularly neat, flat, double flowers of a soft lilac-pink, fading paler and reflexing almost into a ball. I find it one of the most appealing among the Damask roses. Prune after flowering. (See also page 42.)

74

'PARSONS'S PINK' (*above*)

What we know as 'Parsons's Pink' or 'Old Blush China' rose is in reality a very old Chinese Hybrid, grown and recorded over 1000 years ago in Chinese paintings. Perhaps one day we shall find its Chinese name. It reached our shores in 1793 and is a modest little semi-double soft pink flower on a comparatively spindly bush, though capable of sending up good strong shoots bearing many flowers late in the season. It was this priceless attribute which led to its eventual absorption into the strain of European Shrub roses, resulting in Bourbons and Hybrid Perpetuals. It needs good rose soil and a clearing out of small twiggy growths in late winter or early spring. Like 'Mutabilis' (see pages 98–9) it can be trained on warm sunny walls where it may be expected to reach 10ft (3m).

'DUCHESSE D'ANGOULÊME' (*opposite*)

One of the real old favourites, dating from 1836, 'Duchesse d'Angoulême' has a charm all of its own. A charm of delicate, loose, thin-petalled blooms and a charm of a graceful drooping habit. It has good scent and leaves. Its swooning grace demands support from stout stakes and cross bars so that it can flop over as it wishes and still not be stained by splashes from the soil in rain. Or, if you wish to have greater height, so that its delicacy is near eye and nose, have it grafted on stems to make what has become known as a "standard".

Aster thomsonii 'NANUS' (*above*)

Few herbaceous perennials have a longer flowering period than *Aster thomsonii* 'Nanus'. The species itself does not seem to be in cultivation but was brought from western Himalayan regions in 1887. Earlier in this century, when crossed with A. *amellus* it gave rise to A. x *frikartii* of which the cultivar 'Mönch' is the best, and it has inherited from A. *thomsonii* an equally long flowering period. In fact, for providing cool lavender-blue for about three months on end these two asters — they are hardly 'Michaelmas Daisies' since they start to flower in July — are unequalled. 'Nanus' is a short plant, seldom more than 15in (38cm) in height, and slowly increases at the root but is never invasive. It is a wonderful plant for providing soft colour at the end of the summer rose-season and continuing to act as a complement to all the later blooms. It is easily, if slowly, increased by division in spring.

Campanula latiloba 'ALBA' (*opposite*)

In our search for tall, white-flowered perennials to add a touch of lightness to the rounded outlines of the rose bushes we chose *Campanula latiloba* 'Alba'. It has flowers of a particularly clean, gleaming white. It opens just before the Old Roses are at their best and has a season of three or four weeks before it is necessary to cut down the stems for the sake of tidiness. Then is revealed the fact that its basal foliage in the form of handsome rosettes, close on the ground; each rosette takes a season or two to throw up a good flower spike and then dies, its place being speedily filled by young rosettes and they last in green beauty through the winter. In spite of its height — it may achieve 4ft (1.2m) in good soil — it seldom requires support, and being a native of Siberia its hardiness cannot be in question.

'BLAIRII NUMBER 2' (*above and opposite*)

One of the great beauties of the older roses is that the doubles are so filled with petals that they are still shapely and beautiful when full-blown. The same cannot be said of all moderns. In my estimation we need either to see the flower finished, as Nature intended, with an array of yellow stamens, or the flower should be filled with petals. The 'doubling' of a flower, after all, is simply due to the stamens being turned into petals, and as such few doubles would be capable of setting seeds and perpetuating themselves. It has been left to man to search for and find these abnormalities and to cherish and propagate them — such as 'Blairii Number 2' here depicted in its fresh glory.

And what a display we get from 'Blairii Number 2' when its long shoots are allowed to hang out of their support — in this case a pyramid of rustic poles — just at the level of our noses. Mr Blair of Stamford Hill, London, raised his roses around 1845 and they are not surpassed today in their unique early midsummer qualities. The young foliage is coppery and I challenge anyone to pass this by at flowering time; it is a great display every year, with little pruning beyond cutting out old spent wood. It has a delicious scent and a good well-filled shape.

Central Borders after the Main Rose Season

When the main rose season at midsummer is a memory, the central mixed borders continue to provide colour. Here the *Alchemilla* is fading and will soon need all flower stems removing to prevent it from seeding everywhere. Catmint (*Nepeta* x *faassenii*) provides a continuing display but the main interest is from *Agapanthus* Headbourne Hybrids, a selection of hardy perennials which are mainly descended from *A. campanulatus*, a native of South Africa. The soft Wedgwood-blue has a fine complement in the clumps of grey foliage from various pinks and the Seakale (*Crambe maritima*) and the 'Silver Carpet' form of *Stachys byzantina* or Lamb's Ears. All of these plants are of easy cultivation and are best planted in spring. Very soon the standard *Hibiscus syriacus* will be in flower, which will carry us into September.

Geranium 'Mavis Simpson'

I am not sure whether it was a shower of rain or a very heavy dew that decorated so beautifully the new *Geranium* 'Mavis Simpson'. This plant occurred by chance on the rock garden at Kew about 1980, close to plants of G. *endressii* and G. *traversii*, between which it is considered to be a hybrid. From the latter it inherits its silky grey-green leaves, stems and buds, from the former greater hardiness and vigour. In a warm, well drained garden it will flower the summer through, reaching about 1ft (30cm) high and more in width. Divide carefully in spring.

Moss Roses

The Common Moss Rose — *R. x centifolia* 'Muscosa' has been a special favourite since 1727 prior to which date it originated as a sport of *R. x centifolia* itself. In all characteristics it echoes its famous parent except for the mossy excrescences on the bud. It is a lax-grower with good foliage and a wealth of fragrance in its deep-centred flowers. On its right is 'Shailer's White' which occurred in 1790 at Bristol, a direct sport of the Common Moss; this is proved by the fact that every now and again it will produce a normal pink flower. It is, if possible, even more appealing than its parent. Next along the border in this galaxy of colour is the much sought Moss 'Salet' while the near-white is the repeat-flowering 'Mousseline'. At the back is the unique 'Belle Amour' whose colour contains a hint of salmon and whose scent foreshadows the hint of myrrh in 'Constance Spry'. On the corner of the bed on the left is 'Gloire des Rosomanes' of 1825, a rose derived partly from the China Rose. As a consequence it is repeat-flowering and was a foretaste of the rich crimson colouring found in Hybrid Perpetuals later in the century.

'Mrs John Laing'

'Mrs John Laing', raised in England in 1887 and not surpassed in its particular
style of beauty since, in spite of the many that have come and gone. Very rarely
today do we find any rose with so bland a pink, with just a hint of lilac;
practically all pink roses today verge towards the yellow in the spectrum. I was
brought up with 'Mrs John' − my father's favourite rose − so I may be
prejudiced, but in shape, colour and fragrance it stands very high. The slender
incipient hep denotes Damask ancestry. Like many Hybrid Perpetuals it makes
long shoots which, when winter comes, should not be shortened but be tied
down to a neighbouring bush; they will then flower abundantly along their
entire length. Frequent dead-heading promotes later crops.

'Ulrich Brunner Fils'

Raised by Levet in Lyon, France — the raiser of the immense 'Paul Neyron' —
'Ulrich Brunner Fils' (1883) has large, blowsy, but fragrant flowers. It is very
vigorous with good foliage, and if the long summer shoots are pegged down in
winter, as recommended for 'Mrs John Laing', a scene of real splendour will
result. To obtain the best effect from this bending down of branches a low grey
ground-cover is advised, such as *Stachys byzantina* 'Silver Carpet'.

'ROSE DE RESHT'

This rose was found by Nancy Lindsay before World War II in what was then known as Persia. It has been posited that it may well be the old 'Rose du Roi', it is certainly nearly related to the Portland roses, derived from the Damask. It is a rose with recurrent flushes of bloom from midsummer until the autumn. This alone would make it worth growing; coupled with its small, bushy, leafy growth, shapely small flowers and marked fragrance it stands high. The flowers are always beautifully quartered. Regular removal of dead flowers promotes later crops.

Eryngium x *tripartitum*

We have to wait until mid-July for *Eryngium* x *tripartitum* to flower and then it lasts in beauty until all the flowers and spiky bracts are dark blue, but it is lovely even when young and green. It is probably a garden hybrid, and a far better plant with a lower, more compact display than the closely related, taller *E. planum*. It can be staked upright but I prefer it not so tended and allowed to flop forwards, especially if it can flop over the glaucous-white sculptured foliage of *Crambe maritima*, the Seakale. Both love hot sunshine and are best planted in early spring.

'HUGH DICKSON' (*above and opposite*)

Making shoots sometimes 8ft (2.4m) long, 'Hugh Dickson' has been a favourite since its brilliant crimson burst into the rose-world in 1905. It has even been known as 'Climbing Hugh Dickson'. If you train it on a wall or other support, be sure to arrange for as many of the long shoots to be as near horizontal as possible; then will you have a display that has few equals, blooms appearing from every leaf-joint. It has so many assets; unequalled pure colour, rich fragrance from shapely flowers, and good growth. And after the brilliant summer crop you may be sure of a great crop again in September and many odd blooms in between, if you keep it regularly dead-headed. Though classed (rightly) as a Hybrid Perpetual, it brought a beautiful shape that was becoming the prerogative of the Hybrid Teas. Only once, now and again, do we have the best of both worlds.

'DEUIL DE PAUL FONTAINE'

A very dusky rose is 'Deuil de Paul Fontaine' which dates back to 1873. It seldom exceeds 3ft (90cm) and is bushy, with good foliage. The stems and buds are covered with prickly Damask moss and the buds are dense and globular, from very dark reddish maroon through dark Tyrian rose to purple and maroon, often with brown shading. No two blooms are alike. In addition to their rich colours the blooms are usually well quartered and with button eye. Like 'James Veitch' (see page 146) it is not over-endowed with vigour. If the dead blooms are picked off consistently it can well flower from midsummer till October.

90

'GÉNÉRAL SCHABLIKINE'

The best and hardiest Tea and China roses flower early in the rose season, produce a second flush in early August, and after that go on producing until the autumn. There is a delicacy of smooth stems, often flushed with coppery red, smooth leaves and blooms of scrolled shape which we associate with modern roses, and a delicate fragrance. 'Général Schablikine' brings us first to the Tea-China influence; it was raised in 1878 and has a soft, coppery, crimson-pink colouring with a tincture of yellow in the background – inherited from the Tea roses. Constant dead-heading will guarantee continuous flowering and fairly hard pruning in winter is needed to encourage strong young growth.

(*Above*) Along the brick edging of the mixed borders are what we might call large rock plants — plants which are quite at home in the ordinary soil and contribute some early colour, even though their growth is quite small. There are aubrietas and Thrift, campanulas and the pale yellow form of *Alyssum (Aurinia) saxatile* which has such excellent grey foliage for the summer months. *Geranium sanguineum*, our native Bloody Cranesbill in magenta, changes its colour only on the island of Walney off the coast of Lancashire. There one may find pale pinks whose petals are threaded with crimson. Such is *G. s. striatum (lancastriense)*, a worthy small plant for any garden. It may easily be divided in spring.

(*Opposite*) An August picture dominated by the standard *Hibiscus syriacus* 'William R. Smith' in pure white underplanted with the lavender-blue dwarf shrub *Caryopteris* x *clandonensis* 'Arthur Simmonds'. In front of this is *Sedum spectabile* 'Brilliant' with *Aster thomsonii* 'Nanus' while a tall clump of *Perovskia* 'Blue Haze' keeps guard in lavender-blue bloom to the right. This is a grouping which remains in beauty for many weeks and all the kinds are best transplanted in spring and thrive in any well drained soil. It is a rule in these borders that the series of standard hibiscuses are rendered the more important by being backed by a buddleja which is in turn backed by a rambler rose on supports.

'ARCHIDUCHESSE ELISABETH D'AUTRICHE'

Was there ever more voluptuous quartering than in 'Archiduchesse Elisabeth d'Autriche', a rose of 1881? The petals resemble groups of curved shells. The slender incipient hep denotes Damask parentage as it does in most Hybrid Perpetuals. Freely flowering in two good crops, this is a low bush seldom more than 3ft (90cm) high. It has a sport, 'Vick's Caprice', which shows pale striping, but unfortunately is not very stable. Both suffer from wet weather which causes the petals to 'ball'. Pruning as for modern roses.

'REINE DES VIOLETTES'

Born in 1860 and still going strong is the incomparable 'Reine des Violettes'. Although always classed as a Hybrid Perpetual this rose has more in common with the Bourbons, well furnished with smooth, somewhat greyish leaves, making a shapely rounded bush and does not produce the abnormally long new growths associated with most Hybrid Perpetuals. I need say little about the flowers except that with age they expand to a flat array of soft parma-violet, showing the paler, pinker undersides of the petals around the fairly frequent button eye. 'Queen of the Violets'! Today it would have been called 'Queen of the Blues' most likely in an essay of flattery, but no blue could surpass its amazing richness. My experiences of this rose make me add that it must be well nurtured in good soil; it does not take kindly to poor soils. Assiduous dead-heading will encourage later blooms; those which appear late in the season — like this one — surpass the earlier crops in deep colours. A good thinning in winter and reduction of weak shoots is the required pruning.

JAPANESE ANEMONES

Japanese anemones, to me, herald the autumn, but at least we know we shall have them in flower for many weeks, as a rule until mid-October. 'September Charm' (flowering abundantly in the background of this picture) is one of the earliest to flower and leans most towards *A. hupehensis*. It was raised as long ago as 1932 and graces most gardens in August, achieving some 4ft (1.2m) and spreading readily at the root in any fertile soil, preferably in sun or slight shade. It is here growing with *Artemisia ludoviciana* in the foreground and a few *Agapanthus* Headbourne Hybrids tucked in between. None of these plants requires staking, and they are best planted in spring.

Kniphofia caulescens

Most of the Red Hot Pokers or *Kniphofia* are too bright and many of the larger kinds are too tender for Mottisfont. Not so *K. caulescens* which we use as a greyish foliage plant and ground-cover of excellence. Sometimes flowers are borne in summer, sometimes in autumn, according to the season; this clump is flowering in September with Japanese anemones. *K. caulescens* tempers the colour of its flowers to soft tones, soft coral and straw yellow, blending with its foliage. It is a native, like most species of *Kniphofia*, of South Africa.

'MUTABILIS'

An early morning photograph of the China rose bed with 'Mutabilis' at its spectacular best. It is seldom out of flower until the autumn. In cold districts it is apt to suffer in winter but in mild gardens will make huge bushes 8ft (2.4m) high and wide. After the first flush, great new branches arise bearing dozens of the single coppery pink flowers. They turn to light crimson before falling on the fourth day having opened a soft chamois-yellow (as shown in the picture above) from flame buds. It surprises everyone. The small coppery foliage tones in well with the flowers. Thin out all weak twiggy growth in early spring. On the right is 'Parsons's Pink' – what we know as Old Blush China (see also page 75).

Clematis heracleifolia VAR. *davidiana* 'WYEVALE'

These intriguing flowers with their hyacinth-like shape and sweet scent are those of *Clematis heracleifolia* var. *davidiana* 'Wyevale' which I regard as the best of the many forms in cultivation. It takes up a lot of space because it should be allowed to flop on the ground, raising its leafy shoots to about 3ft (90cm), each surmounted by its branching flower-heads. The plants are in flower during August and September. Though it is strictly a herbaceous perennial the annual shoots grow from a firm, hardy, woody rootstock. Where fully established it may cover an area 6ft (1.8m) in diameter. It always attracts attention and is a native of China, whence the species was introduced in 1837. Division or short cuttings in spring.

'LE VÉSUVE'

One of the most satisfactory of the China roses is 'Le Vésuve', which will make a good bush to 4 or 5ft (1.2 or 1.5m) high and wide. It has rather angular growth — though bushy — and large red prickles. The foliage is neat, dark and coppery when young. It would be difficult to imagine flowers of greater charm in their loose shape, warm-coloured in the bud and opening to a soft flesh pink and delicately veined. 'Mutabilis' and this rose require the same treatment and will climb high on a wall. We find 'Le Vésuve' is hardier than 'Mutabilis'. It was raised in 1825. (The spider's web crossing the picture indicates possibly that the insect which ate holes in the rose's petals has been caught.)

'Comte de Chambord' (*above and opposite*)

'Comte de Chambord' of 1860 occupies a unique position not only among the Portland roses but among all roses. Coupled with its sturdy growth, fresh green leaves, gracious double flowers of clear pink and warm fragrance it links the power to flower again and again as the summer advances towards autumn. To those who only know the beauties of the once-flowering Gallicas and their relatives, it is like "eating your cake and having it". It will achieve 4ft (1.2m) and requires repeated dead-heading and the encouragement of a good thinning every winter.

'LOUISE ODIER'

Several of the Bourbon roses excel in the circular arrangement of the petals.
This is 'Louise Odier', a rose of 1851, of good tall growth to about 6ft (1.8m)
and best when given support. On the other hand it will flower most freely when
the long shoots are trained horizontally. It is always bent on producing flowers,
from mid-June to October or later, and they bring rich fragrance to their
charming shape and soft colouring. As with all repeat-flowering roses constant
dead-heading is ideal, to encourage later crops, and a good thinning out of old
twiggy wood in winter is desirable.

Anaphalis cinnamomea, Limonium latifolium, Caryopteris

A late summer combination of the white "everlasting" flowers of *Anaphalis cinnamomea*, a hardy perennial from India and Burma, and a Statice or *Limonium latifolium* selected for its good colour; various good forms are named, such as 'Violetta' and 'Blue Cloud'. The species hails from Bulgaria and South Russia. Neither plant needs any form of support and the group is backed by *Caryopteris*.

HEPS OF RUGOSA ROSES

Although many of the Old Roses bear heps in late summer and autumn they are a comparatively small bonus. Only those which flower once should be allowed to produce a crop; it is important to remove them to encourage later crops on repeat-flowerers. The same rules do not apply to the Rugosa roses here illustrated. The heps are so showy that it is a temptation to leave them on for the brilliance they create, but there is no doubt that they weaken the plants and lessen the later crops of flowers. I try to strike a happy medium in letting heps mature on the single white 'Alba' and on 'Fru Dagmar Hastrup'; this is because I do not like the contrast of orange-red heps with the magenta pinks and crimson forms. 'Fru Dagmar' has light pink flowers and rich crimson heps so all is well.

'FRAU KARL DRUSCHKI'

Apart from being touched with pink in the bud 'Frau Karl Druschki' has petals of snowy whiteness. It was raised in 1901 from a very involved parentage including Tea roses, and thus should be classed as a Hybrid Tea Rose, although usually called a Hybrid Perpetual. In growth and leaf it resembles the latter group, and makes good long growths which are best pegged down. In a good summer there is no white rose so pure and spotless and shapely but alas! it has no scent. It responds to fairly hard pruning in winter.

Sᴡᴇᴇᴛ Bʀɪᴇʀs (*above*)

Behind the seats around the central fountain are placed four Sweet Briers, so that whichever way the wind blows, the sweet apple aroma will reach the seated occupants. This sweetness comes from the viscid leaves. When flowering, further scent comes from the single pink flowers. By September and into the autumn the glittering scarlet heps decorate the bushes, competing successfully with all berried shrubs in brilliance. There are not many shrubs which have such a combination of assets. In the past they were recommended for hedging but the growth is so strong — up to 9ft (2.75m) or more — that they require considerable pruning to keep them in shape. A better plan is to erect metal uprights with crossing wires a foot apart and to tie in all the errant shoots closely. It is one of the most treasured of British wild plants, and also grows throughout Europe and in North Africa. Botanists have called it *R. rubiginosa*, but now adopt the older name of *R. eglanteria*. Shakespeare called it the Eglantine.

(*Opposite*) The birds appreciate the big fleshy heps of *R. rugosa*. Since it is an early flowering rose, the heps begin to colour in August. They are plentiful on all single varieties, but sparing on the doubles. The heps are so large that at the stalk end one can get quite a good bite of red soft flesh — but be careful not to get the hairs around the seeds into the mouth.

108

Colchicum speciosum

By early September the colchicums are in flower. Often called Autumn Crocuses, they are not related to crocuses but have affinity with lilies. "Naked Ladies" is an endearing term for them since they spring up from the ground with no show whatever of leaf. The leaves are large and almost *Aspidistra*-like and burst out of the ground in spring, giving good rich green to assort with daffodils. This is *Colchicum speciosum*, one of the larger species; the white form 'Album' is specially magnificent. They are quite easy to grow in any fertile soil and should be planted in July or early August.

'IRÈNE WATTS' AND COLCHICUMS

Having no foliage of their own at flowering time, it is best to plant colchicums among or near silvery or grey foliage with which they assort so well. Here some of the numerous clumps of hybrid pinks which grow all round the garden are in good contrast. Short growing artemisias and *Stachys byzantina* are also admirable for the purpose. The rose is 'Irène Watts', a China variety of 1896, of good repeat-flowering habit.

LATE SEASON BORDERS

In this picture there is a touch of melancholy in the misty soft tints — a foretaste of autumn. *Perovskia* 'Blue Spire', the best Russian Sage, is in the foreground with *Sedum spectabile* and *Aster thomsonii* 'Nanus' immediately beyond. Over the central path there is a large sprawling clump of *Hebe pinguifolia* 'Pagei' to the left. By the brick edging is the rich colour of *Verbena rigida (V. venosa)* whose tuberous roots survive mild winters, backed by feathery grey-green foliage of *Achillea* x *taygetea*, behind which are more *Sedum spectabile* and *Perovskia* 'Blue Spire' and also a white Tobacco Plant. The view beyond is on to one of the small lawns surrounded by roses and pinks.

The Second Rose Garden

Then in that Parly all those powers
Voted the Rose the Queen of flowers.

Robert Herrick, 1591–1674

IT IS NOW TIME to go through the arch into the Second Rose Garden. This area became available in 1982. There were a few old fruit trees, and figs on the walls, and a lawn which had been used for croquet but, unlike the first garden, it had not been well dug and manured over the years. We soon found that it was on a valuable deposit of the splendid path gravel called hoggin with about a foot of poor stony soil on top. An old saying came to my mind: 'If soil grows stones it will grow anything' – and so it proved, especially as there were wide gates which permitted the entry of tractors.

My colleagues and I were very desirous that this new garden should be quite different from the first, and have a fresh impact. This was all the more important because the main ingredients were to be similar. Visitors had had much to put up with from the narrow paths hedged with box – only just wide enough to permit two people to pass each other. We felt the need for making the walks more spacious. There were no established box hedges and were to be no lawns. It would be a lighter, more open garden. Plans were made for mainly straight paths following the line of the walls round the roughly triangular plot, connecting to a central feature by gently curved paths. The plans were approved by the Gardens Panel of the National Trust and moneys were forthcoming from the Southampton and District Centre, the Arun Valley, West Surrey, Isle of Wight Centres, and many other sources.

We had always felt sorry for visitors to the rose garden who might get caught in a storm and resolved on making tiled shelters with seats in two corners of the garden. The main central feature upon which all the curved paths focused was a brick-paved circle, with a series of stout, chamfered oak posts connected by iron hoops – which we call a bower, as in Victorian days. This elegant structure contains an octagonal raised bed held by walls of knapped flints, which makes a back for black-painted traditional iron seats.

The first thing to do was to lay out the paths, giving them low brick edges. The material from old gravel paths which were uncovered was useful for foundations for the new paths. This all entailed a deal of hard labour on the part of the Head Gardener and his slender staff.

114

Acaena caesiiglauca

There is a very large bed near the middle of the Second Garden; stepping stones interplanted with *Acaena caesiiglauca* lead to a small circle of grey granite cobbles planted with the dark green of Thyme and pinks and the whole is surrounded by six wire spheres (see overleaf.)

The natural gravel of the district is rather yellow. I was particularly anxious that on entering the new garden the picture and feeling should be quite different. We resolved therefore on greyish gravel and edges throughout of dwarf lavender. To give height through the borders and beds some four-posted pillars and stout arches were made, to accommodate rambling roses. Some are reinforced with the silvery leafed *Atriplex halimus*. We had inherited some wire-work spheres which have been used to punctuate stepping-stone paths; they have been given grey-leafed ivies with the intent that they shall give similar effect to topiary. Among the stepping-stones *Acaena caesiiglauca* repeats the greyish effect.

Many years ago I had obtained some old rose varieties from the German National Rose Garden at Sangerhausen in East Germany. Their new list contained a fascinating list of old rose names and over several years we were kindly sent collections of varieties. One of my dreams was not realized. Two of the very best of the Old French roses are what we call 'Fantin-Latour' and 'Empress Joséphine' without any foundation; these names do not occur in any of the old French books listed in the bibliography. I hoped they might turn up under their rightful names. But it was not to be and we must continue with these unfounded names. The first was coined by Ruby Fleischmann and the second by Nancy Lindsay. By dint of very careful comparison with our original cultivars (which I had checked many years ago) and with old French and German books, we are now fairly confident that the names we have tally with old descriptions.

Having again a garden of roses of subdued colours the companion planting – upon which so much of the garden's success depends – had to be of the same tints as before, i.e. white, pale yellow, blue and mauve and grey foliage. For height among the white plants the Madonna Lily

115

Hedera helix 'GLACIER'

One of the six wire spheres surrounding the small circle of grey granite cobbles. These spheres are gradually being turned into greyish pieces of topiary by planting them with an Ivy, *Hedera helix* 'Glacier'.

(*Lilium candidum*) was the obvious choice. It promises to do well in the harsh limy soil and loves full sun. Its glistening, pure white trumpets remain supreme among lilies despite the many new hybrids. It is of unsurpassed beauty and fragrance and flowers at the height of the rose season. An equally pure white is found in the stately *Campanula latiloba* 'Alba'; its relative 'Hidcote Amethyst' is a tender colour that blends with all the roses' tints. For true blue there is *Anchusa azurea* – rather overpowering – and *Linum narbonense*, a richly coloured perennial Flax. Another tall plant with grey leaves and white drumstick flowers is *Echinops* 'Nivalis'. Lovely soft silvery grey foils come from *Artemisia absinthium* 'Lambrook Silver' and *A. ludoviciana latiloba*; they are unequalled in their grey-white brilliance. Catmint flows along the base of a wall covered with Hybrid Perpetual roses and by the corner shelters massed blossom of the richly fragrant 'Sanders' White Rambler' cover both wall and sloping banks. The almost prostrate growth does not impede the view of the borders from visitors seated in the shelters. Through these carpets of white stand the fairy globes of mauve stars of *Allium christophii* which used to be called *A. albo-pilosum*.

More silvery touches are from *Hieracium lanatum*, *Anthemis cupaniana*, and the dwarf *Veronica cinerea*. Less silvery, in fact of glaucous or leaden green, are the dramatic leaves of *Helleborus argutifolius* (synonym *H. lividus* var. *corsicus*) and *Iris pallida* in the form known in gardens as *dalmatica*. The latter, unlike other Bearded Irises, remains fresh in its pale glaucous tint

116

Linum narbonense

Rich, warm, lavender-blue from the south European Flax, *Linum narbonense*. It loves a warm sunny spot in well-drained soil and will delight you with its evanescent flowers daily for many weeks in summer. It is easily raised from seeds but extra rich blue forms can be struck from cuttings.

throughout the summer. I know nothing else which gives such stability to a mixed planting and its clear lavender-blue scented flowers are a joy in late spring. To flower with it or soon after is the white Fraxinella or *Dictamnus albus*; we hope it is getting its roots deep in the ground in preparation to throwing up its spikes of elegant flowers; these are followed by its seed pods which on ignition on a hot day earn its name of Burning Bush. As a change from the ordinary Lamb's Ears in the first garden we planted *Stachys byzantina* 'Cotton Boll'; it is a grey-white erect plant of excellence. In addition to the dark purple dwarf lavender hedges we have a good clump of *Lavandula lanata* whose extra grey leaves are topped by soft violet flower-spikes, and also the white form of the so-called Dutch Lavender.

On the far side of the garden the border is overhung by a large Sycamore. Roses are not likely to thrive in this hot sunny place, but we hope that a grey effect will be obtained by some more tolerant shrubs such as the excessively silvery *Elaeagnus angustifolia* var. *caspica*, *Hippophaë*, the bold-leafed *Desmodium praestans*, *Buddleja fallowiana* 'Alba' and *Lonicera splendida*, with various blue and white perennials.

Considerable deliberation went into the planting of the bower. The Head Gardener and his staff spared no effort to achieve good growth and delved and replaced the gravel with topsoil to the depth of 3ft (90cm), with the result that the rambler roses reached well over the arches in the first season. The choice in roses was an alternating planting of 'Bleu

Artemisia absinthium

Few hardy plants have such a fresh silky-grey appearance as Margery Fish's selected form of *Artemisia absinthium*, which she called 'Lambrook Silver'. The *Artemisia* is the Absinthe Wormwood, a native of Britain and elsewhere in Europe. It glories in a hot sunny position and is in beauty from summer until late autumn.

Magenta' and 'Débutante'. The former came originally from the Roseraie de l'Häy, near Paris, and is the most sumptuous of all the crimson-purple ramblers; the latter is a very dainty clear pink variety long treasured at Nymans. These both, of course, flower only at midsummer, but later interest is ensured by planting short standards of 'Little White Pet' under each metal arch and several short growing repeat-flowering roses beneath. 'Little White Pet' — or 'White Pet' as it is often labelled — originated in 1879 as a dwarf sport from 'Félicité Perpétue', raised in 1827. The dwarf roses include 'Her Majesty' of 1885, which has some of the largest pink blooms of any rose; 'Francis Dubreuil', a magnificent dark crimson Tea rose of 1894 and 'Directeur Alphand', a good light crimson. The last two are very fragrant. The whole of this surrounding bed or border is given pleasant relief by an edging of *Dianthus* 'White Ladies' — the improved 'Mrs Sinkins' — and the silvery filigree of *Artemisia canescens*.

On entering this second garden you have passed through the arch in the wall and have been regaled by the sweet smelling honeysuckle *Lonicera japonica* 'Halliana'. This is semi-evergreen and if pruned back in early spring, produces its creamy yellow flowers for three months or more. But on the wall to the left of the inviting door is the climbing Noisette rose 'Desprez à fleur jaune', with also a very long flowering period and remarkable, fruity scent from its clusters of peachy yellow flowers. It was born in 1830, and together with 'Lamarque', is the oldest of these early yellowish hybrids of the Tea roses. Other such treasures in the First Garden are 'Céline Forestier' of 1842 and the well known 'Gloire de Dijon' of 1853, followed by 'Maréchal Niel' in 1864. Of the varieties that have remained all these years in cultivation they are at once the most tea-scented, the most yellow and the most regular in their successive crops of bloom — in fact a well nourished plant should be in flower from mid-June

'FRANCIS DUBREUIL'

Among the short-growing roses around
the foot of the bower are 'Her Majesty',
a wonderful very large pink of 1885
(named, therefore, after Queen Victoria),
'Directeur Alphand', a vivid light
crimson fading to purple of 1883, and
'Francis Dubreuil' of 1894 which is
misleadingly classed as a Tea rose in old
books. It might well be called a Hybrid
Tea: the photograph shows its shape and
pure colour to perfection — but not the
sweet perfume. All of these require dead-
heading to encourage late crops and
winter pruning to keep the plants
vigorous, up to a maximum of 3ft (90cm).

until early autumn, and they owe all these characters to one parent. Thus
these yellow roses set the stage for all the repeat-flowering climbers and
shrub roses and have never been surpassed. They owe all their fame and
prowess to one of the Chinese hybrids which reached us first in 1824,
which we have always called 'Parks's Yellow Tea-scented China' though
doubtless it had a Chinese name; it was introduced by John Damper Parks,
collecting on behalf of the Royal Horticultural Society. It is believed to
be a hybrid between the tea-scented, very vigorous, *Rosa gigantea* — the
Tea Rose — and 'Hume's Blush', already a hybrid with a form of *R.
chinensis*. 'Hume's Blush', introduced in 1809, is probably extinct for the
plant found in gardens under this name is far removed from the gracious
Redouté portrait. The single, palest yellow *R. gigantea* is not hardy at
Mottisfont, but at present grows at Wisley, having been propagated from
a plant at Mount Stewart, a National Trust garden in Northern Ireland.
It is a strong climber and tea-scented.

We are delighted to have acquired from Peter Beales Parks's rose; it
grows on the warmest sunny wall of the second garden. It suffers in cold
winters and seldom flowers but when it does it produces long-lasting, long-
petalled, loose blooms of pale yellow, delicately scented, and a foretaste
of 'Maréchal Niel' which remains in all ways the apotheosis of these
famous Tea roses. The scent of tea, recorded as early as 1848 by William
Paul in *The Rose Garden*, is noticeable at all times of the day and recalls
the aroma from a freshly opened packet. None of these ancient yellow-
toned roses resembles the sharp, strong yellows of roses raised since 1900;

119

they are all of creamy or yolk-yellow with an excursion or two towards sulphur in 'Céline Forestier' and 'Maréchal Niel'; on the other hand 'Lamarque', which grows next to Parks's rose, may best be described as white with a lemon centre.

Among the many fresh varieties of shrub roses planted in the various beds and borders are several invaluable rich purplish cultivars; they are little known but are likely to become popular again because they yield a good second crop of flowers in late summer and early autumn, providing they are dead-headed promptly and soaked if the summer be dry.

Raised in France in 1865 and named after the noted British nurseryman, 'James Veitch', is a very prickly bush of low, compact growth, of Damask-Moss persuasion. The flowers are semi double, of dusky crimson-maroon fading to a strange mauvy tint, with a hint of slaty magenta. It is a useful front-line plant and has been given two prominent corners. There are several fresh Portland varieties, one of which — 'Indigo', raised about 1830 — is the largest and darkest of all this group and makes a fine upstanding, repeat-flowering bush. It is the only large, dark purplish variety listed in old books. It is much larger in flower than 'Pergolèse'. 'Marbrée' of 1858 has clustered heads of light crimson speckled with pink; they open wide and flat. 'Rembrandt' of 1883 is a less compact but upright bush with small flowers of light crimson, raised and blotched with darker tones.

There are also some repeat-flowering roses of the Bourbon group. 'Madame Souchet' was raised in 1843 and brings to the collection a blush-white tint and is therefore doubly valuable. 'Héroïne de Vaucluse' is a dark lilac-crimson, fading paler, with attractive rolled petal-edges. Its date is 1866; three years later 'Souvenir de Madame Auguste Charles' appeared; it is of camellia-like perfection in light pink. There are also some fresh Gallicas and Centifolias. 'Charles Quint' is a neat bush and a useful addition to the striped varieties in pink and lilac. 'Bérénice', a variety of 1818, resembles 'Belle de Crécy', but is of richer colouring and 'Bellard', of 1857, is of clear pink fading to blush or even white at the edges.

The purplish tones stem entirely from *Rosa gallica*. It is a strange fact that, while we now welcome their rich velvety effect, our great-grandparents were always seeking more pure crimson tints which stem only from the China Rose itself, and in the hands of the breeders of the nineteenth century from what we know as 'Slater's Crimson China'. This was growing in England in about 1792 and represents the first glimpse that Europeans had of the potentiality of the China Rose. In the wild this is a large, arching semi-climber with flowers only at midsummer; as is common with climbing roses, dwarf sports or hybrids tend to be perpetual or at least repeat-flowering. *Rosa chinensis* var. *spontanea*, the wild species, is at last in cultivation over here through the kindness of my freind Mikinori Ogisu and it remains to be seen whether it is hardy. 'Slater's Crimson', or

Argemone grandiflora

It is, to say the least, obliging of a poppy, native to South West Mexico to settle down in our gardens and spread itself by seeding. Such is the habit of *Argemone grandiflora* whose grey leaves and white flowers assort so well with our colour schemes. It reaches almost 2ft (60cm) in height.

something very near it, grows in Bermuda, but it is scarcely hardy over here. It is another strange fact that forms of plants with very dark colouring are often weaker growing than those of lighter tint. If we retrace our steps to the bed of China roses in the First Garden, we shall find several roses of true dark crimson. Direct from China in sendings since the end of the eighteenth century is 'Chi Long Han Zhu' which signifies 'with a pearl in red dragon's mouth' and is also known as 'Willmott's Crimson China'. Not far removed from it but with rather larger and fuller flowers, is the old French hybrid 'Cramoisi Superieur' of 1832. Direct from the Bermuda Rose Society is a little plant with startling, small, single intense crimson flowers called 'Sanguinea'. Early in this century E.A. Bowles received from Dr Lowe of Wimbledon another weak grower with single crimson flowers, paler in the centre, which is named 'Miss Lowe'. And then there is Nancy Lindsay's foundling from the south of France which she called, very suitably, 'Bengal Crimson'. This has made a fine bush at Wisley and, like all the others, is constantly in flower. It should be noted that all these roses have flowers of intense dark red but are only faintly scented. The colour darkens with age, which is the wont of *R. chinensis* var. *spontanea* itself. This is the origin of the dark red colouring of our modern roses; the first intimation being the evolution of the Hybrid Perpetual roses in the second half of the nineteenth century, and it is to the new arrivals in this group that I want to devote the next paragraph or two.

'GLOIRE D'UN ENFANT D'HIRAM'

One of the most sumptuous of the Hybrid Perpetuals is a rose of 1899 – 'Gloire d'un Enfant d'Hiram', a big, lax grower with few prickles and good leaves, which is best when trained on wall or fence. There is nothing to touch the size, full shapeliness and glowing crimson tint, bright red in bud, fading slightly purplish with age, but at all times arresting and fragrant. It has at its foot some *Melissa officinalis* 'Allgold', which in the shade of the wall will show a clear light lime-yellow. The rose requires the usual dead-heading and a reduction of all weak, twiggy growth in winter.

Though 'Hugh Dickson' of 1905 has stolen the thunder in the First Garden, the nearest to pure crimson in this the second garden is 'Gloire d'un Enfant d'Hiram' of 1899. This graces a north-facing wall and has for a companion below it the brilliant lime-green of *Melissa officinalis* 'Allgold'. Striving towards these purer crimson varieties are several of a rich, strong purplish tone fading paler: 'Jean Rosencrantz', 1864; 'Duke of Edinburgh', 1868; 'Le Havre', 1872; 'Star of Waltham', 1875 and 'Souvenir de Jeanne Balandreau' of 1879. They all add much rich colour and a fullness of flower to the garden. It is just as well that we have the charming 'Paul's Early Blush' and 'Sidonie' of clear light pink to add contrast. There are several other roses of equally bright colouring in this new garden but I hope I have said enough to indicate the enormous advance derived from breeding with China Rose derivatives.

Most of these Hybrid Perpetuals make long growths and produce the best display when these are tied down to the base of neighbouring bushes, or trained fan-wise on a wall or other support. These long shoots are the very essence of the Hybrid Perpetuals and should be respected and encouraged. It is a mistake to reduce their height to three or four feet (0.9 to 1.2m). The whole beauty of the bush will thereby be lost. When the long shoots are bent downwards or trained nearly horizontally they flower all along their length; if trained vertically they only flower at the top. They are all substantial in flower, foliage and growth and need substantial companions in solid groups.

122

The spring-flowering wallflower known as *Erysimum* 'Bowles' Mauve' lingers in flower into the summer, its tumps of fine leaden grey leaves being a real asset. Of similar colour in leaf is *Lysimachia ephemerum* whose erect stems produce spikes of grey-white flowers at the top. Clear lavender-blue comes in plenty from *Galega orientalis* and *Salvia haematodes*. The former is rather invasive; the latter sometimes short-lived, but it produces plenty of seeds.

Some of the richer, more subdued purplish and mauvy-tinted roses are enlivened by lavender-blue and white flowers or intensified by plantings of clear pink. For the strangely tinted 'James Veitch' Moss Rose we have chosen the comparatively new perennial, *Coreopsis verticillata* 'Moonbeam', a yellow of very delicate hue and long flowering season. I should not want the pretty little *Corydalis lutea* among any but the clearest pinks and whites of the Alba group; it is moreover a tremendous colonizer. On the other hand its close relative *C. ochroleuca* is more compact, less prolific in progeny and is of a cool creamy white. It prefers the shady side of a bush, as does *Dicentra* 'Langtrees', a glaucous-leafed, blush-white variant of special charm.

Of recent years I have been using *Salvia blancoana* in frontal positions, particularly when its prostrate stems can push forward over a low wall, displaying its tiny grey leaves and long sprays of lavender flowers at rose time. Lastly I must give a noted hybrid plant its due. It is *Geranium* x *cantabrigiense*, a hybrid between the splendid rampageous *G. macrorrhizum* and the small delectable rock plant *G. dalmaticum*. The result is a very dense, compact ground-cover of the highest merit for sunny or shady positions, the little rounded, lobed leaves making a dense cushion. The flowers of the original are of a rather muddy mauve, but there is a good blush-white 'Biokovo'.

'DESPREZ A FLEUR JAUNE' (*above*)

The arch in the wall leading into the Second Garden of roses with its low hedges
of lavender. We used seed-raised *Lavandula angustifolia* of which one form is
known as 'Hidcote'. There is very little variation in the plants. Although usually
a reliable grower we are experiencing trouble with a number of plants, deaths
making gaps in the hedges; we may have to adopt instead 'Munstead' lavender,
which grows reliably elsewhere in the garden. *L. angustifolia* was initially chosen
because of its dark violet-blue colouring and extra grey leaves. On the right of
the archway is a species of the Synstylae section of the genus, extremely sweetly
scented and on the left is the long-treasured 'Desprez à fleur jaune' of 1830, a
hybrid, it is recorded, between 'Blush Noisette' and 'Parks's Yellow Tea-Scented
China'. The latter is an ancient garden hybrid from China; 'Blush Noisette' was
raised in South Carolina, a hybrid between 'Parsons's Pink' and *Rosa moschata*
of Europe. Such is the extraordinary far-flung parentage of Desprez's rose. It is
seldom out of flower and an unforgettable scent comes from its peachy-apricot
blooms. It should be thinned out in winter. Synstylae roses, being once-
flowering, should be thinned after flowering only.

(*Opposite*) One of the arches of the bower, central to the paths in the garden,
frames a view towards the corner-shelter and the astrolabe; this has been newly
constructed and given a substantial column to raise it to eye-level. It is an
instrument formerly used for measuring altitudes.

124

THE BOWER

The Bower is constructed of a brick-paved circle, on which stand eight chamfered oak posts, supporting metal arches. The roses 'Blue Magenta' and 'Débutante' are planted on alternate posts. The former is the most sumptuous of all the purplish ramblers, with good foliage, but practically scentless. It reached me many years ago from the Roseraie de l'Haÿ. 'Débutante', of 1902, at first sight reminds one of the well-known 'Dorothy Perkins' but is infinitely more beautiful and delicately fragrant. It has neat dark green foliage and the flower sprays are delightfully set with pale green bracts. The bed that supports these roses runs around the octagon except at the paved entrances and is planted with short-growing, repeat-flowering, historic roses and short standards of 'Little White Pet', and edged with 'White Ladies' pinks. 'Little White Pet' (or 'White Pet') originated in 1879 as a dwarf, repeat-flowering sport of 'Félicité Perpétue', the old rambler, descended from *R. sempervirens*, which occurred in 1827.

126

'Bleu Magenta' (*above*)
'Debutante' (*opposite*)

The richly tinted, but scentless blooms of 'Bleu Magenta'. 'Débutante', rather pale, after a hot day. These two roses should have their old, flowered shoots removed from the base immediately after flowering, in order to encourage strong new shoots which in turn will bear the flowering shoots for the next summer.

'Jacques Cartier' (*above and opposite*)

'Jacques Cartier' (sometimes called 'Marquise Bocella') is one of the most reliable of the repeat-flowering Portland roses, hybrids of the Autumn Damask. The present rose was raised in 1868 and is of particularly sturdy upright growth, very prickly with small thorns, and with long-pointed, fresh green leaves. The extraordinary tightly compacted, deep-centred buds are almost crimson, opening flat and densely filled with short petals, quartered and often with button eye, of a good bright pink. They are as full of scent as of petals. This and 'Comte de Chambord' (see pages 100 and 101) are two essentials for a garden of roses. To encourage new growths during the season, every one of which will bear flowers, prune fairly hard in winter.

131

WEST WALL BORDER

The roses in this picture are mainly Hybrid Perpetuals and Bourbons, some grown as bushes, others trained on the wall. A big wooden cage supports the white 'Bouquet Tout Fait', a long-forgotten Noisette, and below it is a group of *Artemisia absinthium* 'Lambrook Silver', selected by Margery Fish many years ago. The Narbonne Flax shows up well in the foreground.

'Le Havre'

'Le Havre' is a strong growing, floriferous Hybrid Perpetual of 1871. The photograph shows how the main shoot, pegged down almost horizontally to the next bush, has produced a flowering shoot at every leaf-eye. It is a good leafy bush and the flowers have the buxom shape of the best Hybrid Perpetuals. Its early and late crops are prolific and it has a good scent. Dead-head frequently and thin out the smaller growths in winter.

'CRÉPUSCULE'

'Crépuscule' was raised by M. Dubreuil in France in 1904. He had previously
(1884) raised that little charmer 'Perle d'Or' which bids fair to outlast most roses,
like 'Gloire de Dijon' (see page 46). Nobody is raising these exquisite Noisettes
today. 'Crépuscule' is of lax, semi-climbing growth and has been recommended
for hedging, but I think is best with support from a wall. After the summer crop
later flowers appear giving us many tints, a delicious fragrance and good foliage.
Thin out old twiggy growth in January to encourage new basal shoots.

134

Veronica austriaca 'ROYAL BLUE'

Stachys byzantina 'Cotton Boll' resembles the ordinary Lamb's Ears but the flowers themselves are thickly swathed in white 'cotton wool'; in its grey-whiteness it is thus a lovely contrast to the green leaves and pure blue flowers of *Veronica austriaca* (*V. teucrium*) 'Royal Blue'. The latter is one of the several selected forms of the species which is a native of Europe and North Asia; the *Stachys* comes from the Middle East. Both are good hardy perennials of about 18in (45cm) for any sunny spot on well drained fertile soil and bring together the two most desirable tints for a garden of Old Roses.

Linum narbonense

The special feature of this picture is the clump of *Linum narbonense* on the left, a Flax that loves the sun. Behind it is the curious form of *Acanthus spinosus*, long treasured in Ireland by Lady Moore, whose young spring foliage is so densely dotted with cream that it looks quite pale. It is mainly green later and is known as 'Lady Moore'. Catmint lines the wall on which is trained, fanwise to encourage blossom, the Bourbon rose 'Souvenir de Madame Auguste Charles'.

‘Bellard’

‘Bellard’ (sometimes spelt ‘Bellart’) is a Gallica rose of 1857. It is distinguished among the many Gallicas by its pale pink tint, fading to almost white at the edges. The flowers are well filled with petals, quartered and with button eye. It has a rich scent and the heps are showy and hispid. Toning in well with it, *Corydalis ochroleuca* (in the foreground) is a native of Italy but is seldom seen in gardens, its place usually being taken by the much more common yellow *C. lutea*, which is a native of Britain and parts of Europe. They both seed themselves freely but do not hybridize in my experience and both prefer the cool side of bushes rather than the hottest sun. They flower through summer and into autumn.

'SOUVENIR DE MADAME AUGUSTE CHARLES' (*above*)

The Bourbon rose 'Souvenir de Madame Auguste Charles' saw the light of day in 1866, a late but distinguished flourish to the long line of this class of rose. It is a lax grower but not over-vigorous, suitable for low wall or fence but not tall arches. The blooms reach a state of perfection when fully expanded — a dense array of petals folded and quartered and with central green pointel. It is not overdone with fragrance but usually produces a good autumnal crop. Keep removing the dead heads, and thin out small twiggy growth in winter. It is a charmer, all on its own.

'TRICOLORE' (*opposite*)

'Tricolore' was raised about 1840, and has the synonym 'Reine Marguerite'. It is a unique Gallica rose showing three colours — vivid crimson fading to purple on the perimeter of the blooms, with slender white streaks on most of the petals. It is a typical Gallica in its growth and foliage and bears fine cupped blooms, reflexing with age, and has a good scent. Thin out twiggy growth after flowering or in winter, at which time the long ungainly new shoots should be shortened.

139

Stachys byzantina 'Cotton Boll'

All forms of *Stachys byzantina* are valuable garden plants for sunny places on well drained soil. The non-flowering 'Silver Carpet' is a useful low form, but possibly the most striking is 'Cotton Boll' whose flower spikes are densely white-woolly so that the flowers do not win through. Here it is with a dwarf lavender whose dark purple flowers are contrasted by its silvery foliage; it is a form of *Lavandula angustifolia*, a native of the Mediterranean Region and parts of southern Europe.

'LE RIRE NIAIS'

The rose in the foreground came to us as 'Le Rire Niais', which dates back to 1810. Why a rose should raise 'a foolish laugh' is beyond my understanding; we just enjoy its beauty. The graceful growth indicates the Centifolia class, but the flowers, pointed leaves and the paucity of prickles remind one of the Gallicas. The sweetly scented flowers are full of petals, quartered and often have a button eye. Contrast its graceful growth, which needs support, with the fine upstanding bush behind of 'Bellard', a Gallica. With them is the white-flowered form of the Culinary Sage, *Salvia officinalis* 'Albiflora'. Sage has long been cultivated as a herb in Europe and has become naturalized in many warm sunny countries. To keep it bushy, clip over in late spring.

'MAGNA CHARTA'
'GLOIRE LYONNAISE'

One of the corner summerhouses in the Second Garden, embowered in roses. In the foreground are groups of *Campanula latiloba* backed by the rosy-crimson 'Magna Charta' and the white 'Gloire Lyonnaise'. These two roses were raised in 1875 and 1885 respectively and usually provide a good second crop of bloom in early autumn. Both are Hybrid Perpetuals, the first English, the second French. 'Magna Charta' has a rich scent. Higher up in the medley of blooms can be seen the white buds of the Madonna Lily, *Lilium candidum*. Over the tiles sprawls the prolific growth of the rare Chinese hybrid of the Tea Rose, 'Parks's Yellow Tea-scented China', which occasionally flowers.

'Captain Hayward'

'Captain Hayward' was raised in Shepperton in 1894 by Henry Bennett, the creator of several famous roses including 'Mrs John Laing' (see page 84). The Captain is a good strong grower but needs support. Note the excellent foliage. The flowers are typical, rather vulgar Hybrid Perpetual in style, with some scent, and a good autumn crop. The magnificent bright crimson colour was much admired in its day but in hot weather fades to lilac pink tones which, however, assort well with all Old Roses. The loosely formed flowers often show some stamens. The stems will reach 6–7ft (1.8–2.1m) and need to be trained as horizontally as possible to encourage flowering shoots. Constant removal of dead heads will usually ensure later crops and the plants repay a good thinning-out of twiggy wood in winter.

'SANDERS' WHITE RAMBLER'

The rose 'Sanders' White Rambler' is a particularly valuable Wichuraiana
hybrid, inheriting that species' late-flowering habit. Moreover it is extremely
sweetly scented. It is equally good as a ground-cover, or when trained on a
support; here its back branches are attached to the wall though allowed to make
a carpet in the foreground, through which grow the stout stems and globular
heads of violet stars of the ornamental Onion, *Allium christophii* (*A. albopilosum*),
from Turkestan. Also in the picture are the last flowers of the Flax, *Linum
narbonense*, and the leaves of Lady Moore's *Acanthus spinosus* have turned to
their dark, satiny green of summer.

'JAMES VEITCH'

Here is the remarkable low-growing 'James Veitch'. It was raised in France in 1864 and named after the most famous of English nurserymen. It is an excessively prickly and spiny bush up to about 2ft (60cm), branching freely and producing successive crops of bloom through the summer and autumn. The moss is green and prickly denoting Damask influence, which also is the cause of its repeated flowering. It is a useful front-line plant. The flowers soon open widely, of dark crimson-maroon fading to soft, vinous, dusky magenta with slate tints. They are quartered and with button-eyes and have a delicate scent. There is nothing like it. It has not been an easy colour to enhance by companion planting, but we think we have achieved it with the pale primrose-yellow of *Coreopsis verticillata* 'Moonbeam'.

'BELLE VIRGINIE'

Few flowers of any kind offer so pure a white as *Campanula latiloba alba*, a favourite old garden plant whose foliage during late summer, autumn and winter creates good rosettes of dark green on the ground. Its upstanding stems make a strong vertical line rather early in the rose season. The rose 'Belle Virginie' is a Gallica with few prickles, and good bushy growth. Opening from cupped dark pink buds to cupped blooms of rich lilac-pink, they fade paler with age, at all times exhaling a sweet scent. It has all the assets of a Gallica, including the plentiful flowers borne upright. Prune away all flowering wood as soon as the flowers have fallen, and shorten long new shoots to within the shape of the bush in winter.

MADONNA LILY

Lilium candidum, the Madonna Lily as we know it in gardens, is probably a good form selected in times long past, pre-history in fact. In my experience it needs a harsh, limy, strong soil in full sun. When the stems bear aloft the unopened buds, topping the glistening white trumpets offset by yellow stamens and exhaling the rich aroma, no lily can compare with it. Unfortunately its foliage is often wasted and brown by flowering time. The bulbs have a short resting period in late July and early August at which time, and then only, it should be transplanted. Early autumn basal foliage quickly appears and lasts through the winter.

148

'SOUVENIR DE JEANNE BALANDREAU'

'Souvenir de Jeanne Balandreau' was raised in France in the last year of the nineteenth century, and until 'Hugh Dickson' came on the scene in 1905, must have held high place among the bright crimson roses. Its arching branch has been tied down to a peg just behind the clumps of white daisies with their silvery foliage — the Italian *Anthemis cupaniana*. This flowers from late spring until midsummer. It needs pulling to pieces in the spring after a few years when some of the rooted branches will soon make a good clump again. Just beyond it is the Hybrid Perpetual 'Star of Waltham', a compact bush raised in 1875 and renowned for its rich colouring and decisive broad leaves. It is seldom more than 4ft (1.2m) and usually bears a good autumn crop, and is fairly well scented. On supports behind the crimson roses is the Noisette rose 'Bouquet Tout Fait'. The supports might be called "tetrapods" — they are composed of four stout upright posts with cross-bars at intervals and at the top: the top of another can be seen farther along the border. 'Bouquet Tout Fait' is fragrant and free-growing and needs dead-heading during the summer to encourage an autumn crop, and a thinning-out of small wood in winter.

Some Important Points on Cultivation

I T IS ONE THING to design and plant a rose garden but quite another to look after it. To a great extent these stalwart roses at Mottisfont are self-reliant, but they need varied attention through the year. They ought to be dead-headed after the summer crop of flowers but generally, owing to the slender staff, this is confined to those which are due to flower again after midsummer. The removal of old twiggy growth that has flowered in summer is a great help against 'black spot' disease. When time permits some old wood is removed from the base of the bushes. The old French roses usually make strong young shoots during the summer; if these are left at their full length, winds will blow them to and fro during their next summer's flowering time, with resultant damage to the blooms. It is best to reduce them in winter by about one third, so that they are within the general outline of the bush.

The roses that produce second and third crops need to be pruned fairly hard in winter, removing all weak twiggy shoots and reducing others to a good 'eye'. Long new shoots may be reduced as above, but a more effective way of making use of the excess vigour is to bend the shoots down, tying them to the base of a neighbouring bush. The once-flowering ramblers should have their spent wood removed immediately after flowering; this plan is adhered to on all pillars and arches, but usually there is insufficient time to attend to those on walls until the winter, when the repeat-flowering climbers are also pruned, and all new wood is tied back.

Walled gardens provide ideal conditions for the incubation of pests and diseases; without a modicum of chemical control of pests and diseases, most of the roses would be spoilt and much of their beauty lost. During spring and summer sprays are used against aphides and fungal diseases by means of a knapsack sprayer which enables the operator to get all round the bushes. We ring the changes between 'Nimrod T', 'Funginex' and 'Benlate' for 'black spot', with 'Funginex', 'Plantvax' and the newer 'Systhane' for 'rust'. As further alternatives 'Tumbleblite' is used, while 'Tumblebug' or 'Malathion' is occasionally used against aphides. In the United States the last two give way, I understand, to 'Isotox'.

To keep paths free of weeds a very early spring covering of 'Simazine' is applied along those which have brick edges; elsewhere 'Paraquat' is used. Alternatives in the United States would be 'Princep' and 'Kleen-up' respectively. In spring a fertilizer high in potash and phosphate is given which helps to ward off attacks of fungal diseases. As much as possible of the ground is then covered, while moist, with bark-shavings which suppress weeds and help to retain moisture.

Shrub roses of extra lax growth are given wooden supports in the form of three or four uprights connected by horizontals, over which the branches gracefully lie.

In short, rose gardens need a lot of attention, but I hope this book has shown it is well worth while.

Loveliest of lovely things are they,
On earth that soonest pass away.
The rose that lives its little hour
Is prized beyond the sculptured flower.

William Cullen Bryant, 1794–1878

Rose Suppliers, a Select List

AUSTRALIA

Heather & Roy Rumsey, 1335 Old Northern Road, Dural, N.S.W.
Ross Roses, St. Andrew's Terrace, P.O. Box 23, Willunga, S.A. S172.

CANADA

Pickering Nurseries, Inc., 670 Kingston Road (Hwy. 2), Pickering, Ontario.

EUROPE

W. Kordes Söhne, Rosenstrasse 54, 2206 Kleine Offenseth, Sparrieshoop in Holstein, Germany.

NEW ZEALAND

Trevor Griffiths Ltd., No. 3 R.D. Timaru.
Ken Nobbs, Paddy's Road, Te Kauwhata, P.O. Box 10093, Auckland 3.

SOUTH AFRICA

Ludwig's Roses (Pty) Ltd., P.O. Box 28165, Sunnyside, Pretoria 0132.

UNITED KINGDOM

David Austin Roses, Bowling Green Lane, Albrighton, Wolverhampton, WV7 3HB.
Peter Beales Roses, London Road, Attleborough, Norfolk, NR17 1AY.
Gandy's Roses Ltd., North Kilworth, Lutterworth, Leicester, LE17 6HZ.
R. Harkness & Co. Ltd., The Rose Gardens, Hitchin, Herts., SG4 0JT.
Hilliers Nurseries (Winchester) Ltd., Ampfield House, Romsey, Hants., S05 9PA.
John Mattock Ltd., The Rose Nurseries, Nuneham Courtenay, Oxford, OX9 9PY.
Notcutt's Nurseries Ltd., Woodbridge, Suffolk, IP12 4AF.
Roses du Temps Passé, Woodlands House, Stretton, Stafford, ST19 9LG.

UNITED STATES OF AMERICA

Hybrid roses of an appropriate type for each region of the USA are available from reliable local nurseries and garden centers. The species (old or classic) roses other than the native rugosas are harder to find. The first place to look is *The Combined Rose List* by Beverly Dobson (215 Harriman Road, Irvington, NY 10533; 914-591-6736). This valuable book, updated frequently, offers a rating system as to colour, fragrance, hardiness, resistance to disease, etc. It also offers reliable information on sources of supply for each of more than 1000 species, both domestic and foreign nurseries. Also available but without information on

152

sources of supply is the *Handbook for Selecting Roses* from the American Rose Society (Department HB, P.O. Box 30,000, Shreveport, LA 71130). This booklet rates roses by type. Especially helpful are the lists organized by colour, hardiness and type of plant: climbers, shrubs, etc.

The four best-known domestic suppliers are Heritage Rose Gardens (40305 Wilderness Road, Branscombe, CA 95417), Historical Roses Inc. (1657 West Jackson Street, Painesville, OH 44077), Roses of Yesterday and Today (802 Brown's Valley Road, Watsonville, CA 95076) and Wayside Gardens (Hodges, SC 29695-0001).

Table of Companion Plants

=Evergreen, E. Summer=Early Summer, L. Summer=Late Summer

NAME	SEASON OF FLOWERING	COLOUR OF FLOWER OR LEAF	APPROXIMATE HEIGHT OF FLOWERS AND SPREAD	PAGE
aena caesiiglauca	inconspicuous	grey	6in×2ft, (15cm×60cm)	115
anthus spinosus 'Lady Moore'	L. Summer	mauve	4ft×3ft (1.2m×90cm)	136, 145
hillea 'Flowers of Sulphur'	Summer	pale yellow	2½ft×2ft (75cm×60cm)	16, 29
hillea x taygetea, (E)	Summer	pale yellow	18in×18in (45cm×45cm)	112
apanthus Headbourne Hybrids	L. Summer	blue/white	2–3ft×2ft (60–90cm×60cm)	16, 80, 96
chemilla mollis	Summer	pale yellow	18in×2ft (45cm×60cm)	17, 32, 48
ium christophii	E. Summer	amethyst	2ft×18in (60cm×45cm)	116, 145, 149
ssum saxatile 'Citrinum', (E, grey)	Spring	citron yellow	1ft×2ft (30cm×60cm)	15, 93
aphalis cinnamomea	L. Summer	white	2ft×18in (60cm×45cm)	105
aphalis triplinervis	L. Summer	white	1ft×18in (30cm×45cm)	16
chusa azurea	E. Summer	blue	3ft×2ft (90cm×60cm)	116
emone 'September Charm'	L. Summer	pink	3ft×2ft (90cm×60cm)	16, 96

153

Anthemis cupaniana, (E, silver)	Spring/E. Summer	white	1ft×2ft (30cm×60cm)	
Aquilegia, Long Spurred	E. Summer	various	2½ft×18in (75cm×45cm)	20,
Argemone grandiflora, (annual)	Summer	white	2ft×1ft (60cm×30cm)	
Armeria maritima 'Laucheana', (E)	Spring	dark pink	9in×1ft (23cm×30cm)	19,
Artemisia absinthium 'Lambrook Silver', (E, grey)	Summer	grey	18in×2ft (45cm×60cm)	116, 1
Artemisia canescens, (silver)	Summer	yellowish	18in×18in (45cm×45cm)	
Artemisia ludoviciana	L. Summer	grey	2ft×2ft (60cm×60cm)	
Artemisia ludoviciana latiloba	Summer	grey	2ft×18in (60cm×45cm)	
Aruncus dioicus	E. Summer	cream	6ft×3ft (1.8m×90cm)	17, 32,
Aster thompsonii 'Nanus'	L. Summer	lavender-blue	1ft×1ft (30cm×30cm)	16, 93,
Atriplex halimus, (E, grey shrub)	inconspicuous	grey	8ft×8ft (2.4m×2.4m)	
Aurinia, see *Alyssum*				
Bergenia cordifolia 'Purpurea', (E)	Spring	magenta	18in×18in (45cm×45cm)	
Buddleja fallowiana 'Alba', (shrub)	L. Summer/ Autumn	white	7ft×5ft (2.1m×1.5m)	
Buddleja 'Lochinch', (shrub)	L. Summer	lavender	8ft×5ft (2.4m×1.5m)	
Campanula alliariifolia	Summer	white	2½ft×2ft (75cm×60cm)	21,
Campanula carpatica	E. Summer	blue/white	10in×1ft (25cm×30cm)	
Campanula latiloba 'Alba', (E)	E. Summer	white	3ft×2ft (90cm×60cm)	77,
Campanula latiloba 'Hidcote Amethyst', (E)	E. Summer	amethyst	3ft×18in (90cm×45cm)	
Campanula persicifolia, (E)	E. Summer	blue/white	3ft×18in (90cm×45cm)	21, 35,
Carnation, Clove, (E)	L. Summer	crimson	1ft×18in (30cm×45cm)	16,
Caryopteris x *clandonensis* 'Arthur Simmonds', (shrub)	L. Summer	lavender-blue	3ft×3ft (90cm×90cm)	
Catmint, see *Nepeta*				
Centaurea hypoleuca 'John Coutts'	E. Summer	pink	1ft×18in (30cm×45cm)	
Centaurea macrocephala	Summer	yellow	4ft×2ft (1.2m×60cm)	
Centaurea ruthenica	Summer	pale yellow	3ft×2ft (90cm×60cm)	

phalaria gigántea	E. Summer	pale yellow	7ft×5ft (2.1m×1.5m)	17, 23
matis heracleifolia 'Wyevale'	L. Summer/ Autumn	blue	3ft×4ft (90cm×1.2m)	16, 100
chicum speciosum	L. Summer	pink	1ft×6in (30cm×15cm)	110
reopsis verticillata 'Moonbeam'	Summer	light yellow	18in×18in (45cm×45cm)	123
rydalis ochroleuca	E. Summer/ Autumn	white/yellow	1ft×18in (30cm×45cm)	123, 137
mbe cordifolia	E. Summer	white	7ft×6ft (2.1m×90cm)	16, 23
mbe maritima	E. Summer	white	2ft×2ft (60cm×60cm)	66, 80
cosmia crocosmiiflora 'Citronella'	L. Summer	citron	2ft×1ft (60cm×30cm)	16, 19
nara cardunculus, (grey leaves)	Summer	violet	7ft×4ft (2.1m×1.2m)	17
ylilies, see Hemerocallis				
modium praestans, (grey shrub)	L. Summer	purple	8ft×8ft (2.4m×2.4m)	117
nthus Highland Hybrids (E)	E. Summer	various	1ft×18in (30cm×45cm)	43, 51, 58
nthus 'White Ladies', (E, grey)	Summer	white	9in×1ft (23cm×30cm)	118
entra 'Langtrees', (grey)	E. Summer	blush	18in×2ft (45cm×60cm)	123
italis grandiflora, (E)	E. Summer	pale yellow	3ft×2ft (90cm×60cm)	21, 30, 54
italis purpurea 'Albus', (E)	E. Summer	white	6ft×3ft (1.8m×90cm)	21, 30, 54, 57
tamnus albus	E. Summer	white	3ft×2ft (90cm×60cm)	117
inops 'Nivalis'	L. Summer	white	4ft×2ft (1.2m×60cm)	116
inops ritro	L. Summer	blue	6ft×3ft (1.8m×90cm)	16
eagnus angustifolia caspica, (grey ub)	E. Summer	cream	8ft×8ft (2.4m×2.4m)	117
eron 'Quakeress', (E)	Summer	lilac	18in×18in (45cm×45cm)	19, 24, 37
ngium x tripartitum	L. Summer	blue	2ft×2ft (60cm×60cm)	16, 87
simum 'Bowles' Mauve', (E)	E./L. Summer	lilac	2ft×3ft (60cm×90cm)	122
endula vulgaris 'Plena'	E. Summer	creamy	18in×18in (45cm×45cm)	44
, see Linum				
ega orientalis	E. Summer	lavender-blue	3ft×2ft (90cm×60cm)	123

Geranium x cantabrigiense	E. Summer	mauve	1ft×2ft (30cm×60cm)	
Geranium x cantabrigiense 'Biokovo'	E. Summer	blush	9in×18in (23cm×45cm)	
Geranium 'Mavis Simpson'	Summer/ Autumn	pink	1ft×2ft (30cm×60cm)	
Geranium sanguineum striatum	Summer	pink	9in×1ft (23cm×30cm)	
Geranium wallichianum 'Buxton's Variety'	L. Summer/ Autumn	blue	18in×3ft (45in×90cm)	
Gypsophila paniculata	Summer	white	3ft×3ft (90cm×90cm)	
Hebe pinguifolia 'Pagei', (E, grey)	E. Summer	white	1ft×3ft (30cm×90cm)	
Hedera helix 'Glacier', (E, greyish ivy)				
Helictotrichon sempervirens, (grass)		grey leaves	4ft×2ft (1.2m×60cm)	
Helleborus argutifolius (E)	Spring	green	2ft×3ft (60cm×90cm)	
Helleborus corsicus, see H. argutifolius	Summer	orange-red	4ft×2ft (1.2m×60cm)	
Hemerocallis fulva 'Kwanso Flore Pleno'				
Hesperis matronalis	E. Summer	pale	3ft×2ft (90cm×60cm)	
Hibiscus syriacus, (shrub)	L. Summer	various	8ft×8ft (2.4m×2.4m)	16, 19,
Hyssopus officinalis	Summer	various	2ft×2ft (60cm×60cm)	
Iris 'Flavescens'	E. Summer	pale yellow	2½ft×1ft (75cm×30cm)	
Iris 'Iris King'	E. Summer	yellow/brown	2ft×1ft (60cm×30cm)	
Iris 'Ochraurea'	E. Summer	white/yellow	4ft×15in (1.2m×38cm)	12,
Iris pallida	E. Summer	lavender-blue	3ft×1ft (90cm×30cm)	
Knautia macedonica	Summer	crimson	2ft×3ft (60cm×90cm)	16,
Kniphofia caulescens, (E)	E/L. Summer	coral	2½ft×2ft (75cm×60cm)	15,
Lady's Mantle, see Alchemilla				
Lamb's Ears, see Stachys				
Lavandula angustifolia, (E, grey)	Summer	purple	18in×18in (45cm×45cm)	124,
Lavandula lanata, (E, grey)	Summer	violet	2ft×2ft (60cm×60cm)	
Lavatera cashmiriana	Summer	pink	5ft×3ft (1.5m×90cm)	

Salvia nemorosa 'East Friesland'	Summer	purple	18in×18in (45cm×45cm)	
Salvia officinalis 'Albiflora', (E)	Summer	white	2ft×2ft (60cm×60cm)	
Salvia officinalis 'Purpurascens', (E)	Summer	violet	2ft×2ft (60cm×60cm)	24,
Saponaria ocymoides, (E)	E. Summer	pink	9in×2ft (23cm×60cm)	15
Scabiosa caucasica	Summer	lavender-blue/ white	2ft×2ft (60cm×60cm)	
Sedum spectabile 'Brilliant'	L. Summer	pink	15in×18in (38cm×45cm)	93,
Sisyrinchium striatum	E. Summer	straw	18in×18in (45cm×45cm)	13, 32, 48
Stachys byzantina, (E, grey)	Summer	grey	18in×2ft (45cm×60cm)	16, 32
Stachys byzantina 'Cotton Boll', (E, grey)	Summer	grey	18in×2ft (45cm×60cm)	117,
Stachys byzantina 'Silver Carpet', (E, grey)	Summer	grey	8in×2ft (20cm×60cm)	
Stachys macrantha, (E)	Summer	pink	2ft×2ft (60cm×60cm)	
Stopkesia laevis	Summer	lavender-blue/ white	1ft×1ft (30cm×30cm)	
Tanacetum coccineum 'Eileen May Robinson'	E. Summer	pink	18in (45cm)	
Veratrum nigrum	Summer	chocolate	5ft×2ft (1.5m×60cm)	17
Verbena rigida	L. Summer	purple	1ft×1ft (30cm×30cm)	
Veronica austriaca 'Royal Blue'	E. Summer	blue	1ft×1ft (30cm×30cm)	12,
Veronica cinerea, (E, grey)	E. Summer	blue	6in×9in (15cm×23cm)	
Veronica longifolia	Summer	blue	4ft×2ft (1.2m×60cm)	

158

Index of Roses